The Women's Institute

cooking from the

garden

the**WI**
INSPIRING WOMEN

SIMON &
SCHUSTER
ILLUSTRATED

London · New York · Sydney · Toronto · New Delhi
A CBS COMPANY

Sara Lewis

First published in Great Britain
by Simon & Schuster UK Ltd, 2012
A CBS Company

Copyright © WI Enterprises 2012

Simon & Schuster Illustrated Books,
Simon & Schuster UK Ltd, 1st Floor,
222 Gray's Inn Road, London WC1X 8HB

www.simonandschuster.co.uk

Simon and Schuster Australia, Sydney
Simon and Schuster India, New Delhi

1 3 5 7 9 10 8 6 4 2

Editorial Director: **Francine Lawrence**
Senior Commissioning Editor: **Nicky Hill**
Project Editor: **Nicki Lampon**
Designer: **Richard Proctor**
Food Photographer: **William Shaw**
Stylist and Art Direction: **Tony Hutchinson**
Home Economist: **Sara Lewis**
Commercial Director: **Ami Richards**

Colour reproduction by Dot Gradations Ltd, UK
Printed and bound in China

A CIP catalogue for this book is available
from the British Library

ISBN 978-0-85720-860-6

Notes on the recipes

Both metric and imperial measurements have been
given in all recipes. Use one set of measurements
only and not a mixture of both. Spoon measures are
level and 1 tablespoon = 15 ml, 1 teaspoon = 5 ml.

Preheat ovens before use and cook on the centre
shelf unless cooking more than one item. If using
a fan oven, reduce the heat by 10–20°C, but check
with your handbook.

Medium eggs have been used.

This book contains recipes made with nuts. Those
with known allergic reactions to nuts and
nut derivatives, pregnant and breast-feeding
women and very young children should
avoid these dishes.

For my father, who always encouraged
me to garden when I was a small child and
who last year helped me expand my own
vegetable garden.

Many thanks to Ann Luxford from the Crawley
Down Allotment and Gardens Association.

Contents

Introduction

Growing your own vegetables has always been popular, but there now seems to be increased interest with long waiting lists for allotments. However, if you don't have an allotment you can still grow your own fruit and vegetables, just on a smaller scale. Why not forfeit an area of lawn or enlarge a flower bed and move the ornamental plants, so creating space for a vegetable garden?

If space is tight, grow vegetables in and amongst the flower beds – a tepee of runner beans can be squeezed in a 60 cm (2 ft) square, a row of peas can be grown near a fence, or lettuces will fit towards the front of a border. If outside space is small, grow vegetables in pots, in a grow bag on a balcony or even in a window box on a wide windowsill.

Growing your own produce means that you can decide what varieties to grow, when to harvest and whether to be organic or not. Nothing tastes better than a home-grown strawberry or just-podded pea, ripened naturally by the sun and eaten just after picking.

It's also a brilliant way to encourage children to learn about where their food comes from; planting seeds is fun and incredibly rewarding, and children are more likely to try different vegetables if they have helped to plant and harvest them.

For experienced gardeners, we hope that the recipes will offer a new twist on familiar favourites, plus introduce you to some new ones to share with family and friends. The amount your crops produce will vary, so use these recipes as a starting point. If you find you don't have quite enough of one thing, perhaps fresh peas, make up the amount with some baby broad beans, and so on.

Getting started

For those new to gardening, the secret is not to be overambitious. Start small and, as you have success, widen your repertoire of fruit and vegetables. Start with just a few packets of seeds to begin with and see how you get on – mixed salad leaves grow quickly, as do runner beans, peas and spinach.

Seed trays are cheap and essential to get your seeds started, and you will need a grow bag or bag of potting compost. Alternatively, recycle washed yogurt pots, large cans or empty paint pots, but make sure you add some drainage holes. You will also need to label your trays. Either buy ready-made labels or again improvise with recycled lolly sticks or strips cut from an old cleaned yogurt pot or milk carton. Label with an indelible marker pen (there's nothing worse than the name of what you were growing disappearing so you have to guess what it is!).

Bringing on your seeds
Do this in trays on the kitchen or garage windowsill, or in a greenhouse or plastic canopied patio mini greenhouse. Once grown, you can pot your seedlings on to recycled flower pots, large washed cans or milk cartons, or even Wellington boots or an old leaky watering can – just remember to add drainage holes. Wooden fruit trays that are often thrown away from greengrocers also work well. Line them with a plastic carrier bag and place some newspaper on the bottom if the base is slatted.

Once your seeds have grown and are large enough to go outside, a good spade and fork are essential to prepare the ground in the veg patch. A rake to level the soil and a hoe to weed around the plants once transplanted are also useful. You'll need stakes and string for supporting tall plants, some form of pest control to keep the slugs and snails at bay and a watering can with a rose so that seeds are moistened rather than waterlogged. Additional extras, such as some fleece or a plastic cloche, can prove invaluable if a late frost is predicted. Fine netting is helpful to stop your precious harvest being eaten by the birds or squirrels.

Digging over your patch
Getting soil ready for planting always takes longer than you think, and it is important not to cut corners. Time spent digging over your vegetable patch and weeding carefully can save time once your vegetables are established. Depending on your soil type and quality, you may need to enrich it with well-rotted compost or manure, or improve drainage if you have a heavy clay base. Once prepared, cover the soil with old pieces of carpet or black plastic sheeting to stop the weeds growing before your seedlings are ready to transplant.

Getting the most from your veg patch
Try to plan a succession of vegetables all year round. For the kind of vegetables that do not keep, sow just a few seeds at intervals and aim to sow every 2–3 weeks. Sow only one or two rows of peas at a time and follow with later varieties. Read the back of the seed packs carefully so that you can plant vegetables suitable for different times of the year.

If you have a tiny garden where space is at a premium, avoid vegetables that take up a lot of space and are relatively cheap in the shops. Rather than growing

starter plants. These are great if time is short, but there is something immensely rewarding about growing your own plants from seed, and they're cheaper too.

Don't scrimp on the watering

Regular watering is the key, and for young plants a watering can or hose pipe with a fine rose is essential to moisten the plants without drowning them. You will need to water more frequently if your soil is sandy, quick-drying soil rather than heavy, moisture-retaining clay. During the height of summer a water butt, or several, are essential. Try to position them near your vegetable patch so that you don't have to walk too far with a full watering can.

Making the most of your produce

Even with the most careful planning you will probably have more of some fruits and vegetables than you can eat at any one time. Try trading with friends and neighbours – they may well have different gluts so you can swap produce. The freezer can be invaluable – it might sound rather old fashioned but it is such a shame not to make maximum use of your produce.

Blanching

Blanching part cooks vegetables so that their quality is not impaired by freezing. It is most useful for green vegetables that go off quickly. Choose young tender vegetables, wash well and cut into small

even-sized pieces. Blanch in batches, no more than 450 g (1 lb) at a time, by adding to a wire blanching basket and lowering into a large saucepan of boiling water so that they are completely immersed. It is important that the water comes back to the boil quickly. Cook for ½ minute for delicate mange tout, 1 minute for peas and 3–5 minutes for thicker stemmed beans or broccoli. As soon as they are just tender, lift the vegetables out of the water, drain well and plunge into a bowl of cold water chilled with ice cubes. Chill for the same time as the blanching time. Several batches of vegetables can be done in the same boiling water, but the cold water will need changing each time. Drain the vegetables and either open freeze until firm on a baking tray and then transfer to a plastic bag or container, or pack directly into a bag. Seal, label and date.

potatoes, courgettes or cucumbers, choose more unusual salad leaves such as rocket, lamb's lettuce or mizuna; brown tinged oakleaf or red tinged lettuces; yellow, purple or speckled beans instead of the more usual green ones; or rainbow chard with their fabulously coloured pink, red and yellow stems instead of spinach. To make full use of ground space, sow quick-to-mature vegetables, such as spinach, radishes or lettuces, between slow-growing ones, such as leeks or winter cabbages. Strawberries needn't be grown in the veg patch but can be planted into hanging baskets or specially designed plastic towers.

Starter plants

To meet the growing interest in growing your own vegetables, more garden centres are now stocking a wide range of

Using gluts

Soups are quick and easy to make in large quantities and great for gluts of tomatoes, carrots, pumpkin, broccoli and courgettes. Pack into single or double portion bags for greater flexibility.

Stew bases are useful to add to mince for a shepherd's pie, chilli or lasagne, or to diced meat for stews, curries and pies. Dice and fry tomatoes, squashes and root vegetables with chopped onions, herbs, spices or garlic and a little stock. Cool and pack into two or four portions.

Tomatoes are best made up into a basic tomato sauce with fried onions, garlic and herbs and then cooled and packed into a plastic bag. Defrost and add to cooked pasta, browned meat for a stew or mixed vegetables for a quick soup.

Orchard fruits are best lightly cooked in a sugar syrup and then frozen in

handy-sized portions as the base for a fruit crumble or pie. Pack in family-sized bags rather than one large one and make sure you label all produce clearly.

Whatever you freeze, try to use up the current stocks before the next year's harvest or the taste and texture will not be so good.

Storing

For large quantities of apples and pears, wrap the fruit separately in newspaper and store in cardboard or wooden boxes with sheets of newspaper between the layers.

Allow newly dug potatoes and carrots to dry off a little outside – don't worry about leaving on a little soil.

Swede, turnips and celeriac are best stored on a wooden rack and loosely covered with newspaper to avoid wet rot. Beetroot can be stored in sharp sand. Leave parsnips in the ground unless the soil is very wet.

Pumpkins can be tricky to store. They need curing, or the skins to toughen up indoors in the warm before they are transferred to a cool airy shed. Turn them from time to time.

Onions, shallots and garlic need to be laid in a single layer on a meshed surface and left to dry outside for a few days. Once dry, tie together or store in a mesh bag in the dark.

Store harvested produce in a cool, dry, frost-free shed or garage and remember to check on your harvest from time to time and use those that are going a little soft or wrinkled first.

Tie bunches of herbs, such as thyme, rosemary or bay leaves, with string and hang in the kitchen, garage or a shed until dry (14–21 days), loosely covered with muslin or paper bags so that they don't get dusty. Keep the bunches small or they could become mouldy in the middle. When dry, pack into small jam jars. Fleshy herbs, such as chives and parsley, are best chopped and then frozen, while stronger tasting herbs, such as basil, tarragon and dill, can be used to infuse bottles of oil or vinegar. Herb flowers can be frozen in sections of an ice cube tray as a pretty addition to a winter drink.

Summer salads

One of the many joys of growing your own vegetables is to be able to go into the garden and pick just a few mixed salad leaves.

Serves 4
Preparation time:
  10 minutes

115 g (4¼ oz) **mixed salad leaves**
150 g (5½ oz) **cherry tomatoes**, halved, or larger **tomatoes**, diced
55 g (2 oz) **radishes**, sliced
3 **spring onions**, sliced, or 1 **shallot**, thinly sliced
Dressing (see recipe)
a small bunch of fresh **herbs**
a few **chive, borage, marigold** or **nasturtium flowers** (optional)

Wash the mixed salad leaves with cold water, drain and pat dry with a clean tea towel or whizz briefly in a salad spinner. Tear any large leaves into pieces and add to a salad bowl with the tomatoes, radishes and spring onions or shallot.

Drizzle with your chosen dressing and then sprinkle with the chopped herbs and flowers, if using.

Dressing
Just choose your dressing from the recipes below and add to taste. Any remaining dressing can be stored in the jar in the fridge for 3–4 days.

Classic vinaigrette
Add 4 tablespoons of olive oil, 1 tablespoon of white or red wine vinegar, 1 teaspoon of Dijon mustard, 1 teaspoon of caster sugar and a little salt and pepper to a jam jar, screw on the lid and shake together.

Honey mustard
Add 4 tablespoons of olive oil, 1 tablespoon of sherry vinegar, 2 teaspoons of runny honey, 1 teaspoon of wholegrain mustard and a little salt and pepper to a jam jar, screw on the lid and shake together.

Roasted garlic & balsamic vinegar
Heat 2 tablespoons of olive oil in a frying pan, add 2 sliced garlic cloves and fry until golden. Leave to infuse for 15 minutes and then strain the oil into a jam jar. Add 2 extra tablespoons of olive oil, 1 tablespoon of balsamic vinegar, 1 teaspoon of light muscovado sugar and a little salt and pepper. Screw on the lid and shake together.

Italian herb
Add 4 tablespoons of olive oil, 1 teaspoon of pesto, the juice of ½ a lemon, 2 finely chopped garlic cloves and a little salt and pepper to a jam jar, screw on the lid and shake together.

Blue cheese & chive
Cut the rind from 85 g (3 oz) of mild creamy blue cheese and mash the cheese in a bowl. Mix in 85 g (3 oz) of fromage frais, 2 tablespoons of milk and a little salt and pepper and then stir in a small bunch of chopped chives.

Yogurt & herb
Place 150 g (5½ oz) of natural yogurt in a liquidiser with a small bunch of mixed herbs, the grated rind of ½ a lemon and a little salt and pepper. Blitz until smooth.

Hot lettuce

It might sound a little weird, but cooked lettuce is surprisingly good. Serve with grilled fish, chicken or meat, or with the Sunday roast.

Serves 4
Preparation time:
   5 minutes
Cooking time:
   10 minutes

200 g (7 oz) **peas**
175 g (6 oz) **lettuce leaves**, thickly sliced
25 g (1 oz) **butter**
4 **spring onions**, thickly sliced
½ teaspoon **caster sugar**
1 tablespoon chopped fresh **mint**, plus extra to garnish
3 tablespoons **crème fraîche**
salt and freshly ground **black pepper**

Add the peas to a saucepan of boiling water and cook for 3 minutes. Drain into a colander. Wash and dry the lettuce leaves.

Meanwhile, heat the butter in a frying pan, add the spring onions and fry for 2 minutes until just softened. Add the drained peas and the lettuce and cook for 2 minutes until the lettuce has just wilted.

Stir in the sugar, mint and crème fraîche. Season lightly and cook over a low heat until the crème fraîche is warmed. Spoon into a warmed serving dish and garnish with the extra mint leaves.

Tip The key is to cook the lettuce briefly for just a matter of minutes until only just wilted.

Lettuce wrappers

We all think of lettuce as an integral part of a salad, but perhaps not as a holder. Serve as a tasty starter or light lunch with warm crusty bread.

Serves 4 as a starter, 2 as a light lunch
Preparation time: 15 minutes
Cooking time: 15 minutes

250 g (9 oz) frozen **chicken livers**, defrosted
1 tablespoon **olive oil**
15 g (½ oz) **flaked almonds**
25 g (1 oz) **butter**
1 small **onion**, chopped
2 **garlic cloves**, finely chopped
2 tablespoons **raisins**
4 tablespoons **medium sherry**
125 ml (4 fl oz) **chicken stock**
salt and freshly ground **black pepper**
8 **Little Gem lettuce leaves** or small **Romaine lettuce leaves**

Put the chicken livers into a sieve or colander, rinse with cold water and drain well. Tip on to a chopping board, cut away any white cores and roughly chop.

Heat a little of the oil in a frying pan, add the flaked almonds and fry until golden. Scoop out of the pan and reserve.

Add the rest of the oil and the butter, heat, add the onion and fry for 5 minutes, stirring until softened and just beginning to brown around the edges. Add the garlic and chicken livers and cook over a high heat for 3 minutes, stirring until browned.

Add the raisins, sherry, stock and a little seasoning and cook for 3–4 minutes until the sauce has reduced slightly and the livers are just cooked with just a hint of pink.

Wash and dry the lettuce leaves and arrange on a plate. Spoon a little of the chicken liver mixture into the centre of each leaf and sprinkle with the almonds. Serve immediately.

Tip Webbs Wonder or Iceberg lettuces make more rounded cup-like containers. If using this type of lettuce, use just 4 leaves.

Variation If you are not a fan of chicken livers then use boned diced chicken thighs or boneless diced chicken fillets instead and increase the cooking time.

Lettuce & herb soup

However much you try to sow lettuce in rotation there are always some that just get too big. They make a great soup, served with good bread.

Serves 4
Preparation time:
  15 minutes
Cooking time:
  25 minutes

50 g (1¾ oz) **butter**
1 small **onion**, finely
  chopped
250 g (9 oz) **baking potato**,
  peeled and diced
750 ml (1¼ pints) **vegetable**
  or **chicken stock**
225 g (8 oz) **lettuce leaves**
50 g (1¾ oz) fresh **parsley** or
  chives with a sprig or two
  of fresh **mint** or **tarragon**,
  roughly chopped
1 teaspoon **caster sugar**
salt and freshly ground
  black pepper
120 ml (4 fl oz) **double cream**
  (optional)

Heat the butter in a large lidded saucepan, add the onion and potato, toss them in the butter, cover the pan and cook gently for 10 minutes, stirring from time to time until softened and just beginning to colour.

Pour in the stock, bring to the boil, cover and simmer for 10 minutes until the potato is tender.

Wash and drain the lettuce leaves and then tear into thick slices. Add to the saucepan with the herbs, sugar and a little seasoning. Simmer for 2–3 minutes until the lettuce has just wilted.

Purée in batches in a food processor or liquidiser until smooth and then return to the saucepan. Taste and adjust the seasoning if needed.

Reheat, ladle into bowls, swirl a little cream on the top of each bowl, if using, and serve.

Radish tzatziki & meatballs

Don't be put off by the list of ingredients. Serve with home-made flatbreads or, if you are short of time, cheat and serve with pitta breads.

Serves 4
Preparation and cooking time:
   55 minutes

salt and freshly ground **black pepper**
2 large handfuls **mixed salad leaves**, to serve
Flatbreads (see recipe)

Radish tzatziki
200 g (7 oz) **radishes**, thinly sliced
200 g (7 oz) **Greek** or **natural yogurt**
2 tablespoons chopped fresh **mint**

Meatballs
1 **onion**
2 **garlic cloves**
500 g (1 lb 2 oz) lean **minced lamb**
1 teaspoon **smoked paprika**
1 teaspoon **cumin seeds**, roughly crushed
1 **egg yolk**
2 tablespoons **olive oil**

For the tzatziki, mix the radishes with the yogurt, mint and a little seasoning in a bowl.

For the meatballs, finely chop the onion and garlic in a food processor, add the mince, spices, egg yolk and seasoning and mix together well. If you don't have a food processor, finely chop the onion and garlic by hand and then mix with the remaining ingredients. Shape into 32 small meatballs and thread loosely on to 8 metal skewers.

Brush the meatballs with a little oil and then grill or barbecue for 12–15 minutes, turning the skewers several times until the meat is cooked through and evenly browned. To double check, cut one of the meatballs in half; if they are still a little pink, cook for a few more minutes until brown all the way through.

Serve the tzatziki with a handful of salad leaves, two meat skewers each and warm Flatbreads.

Tip Tzatziki can also be made with roasted and grated beetroot with a few chopped walnuts; lightly fried sliced courgettes in olive oil flavoured with thyme leaves; or lightly cooked spinach, each mixed with yogurt as above, seasoning and, for garlic fans, a crushed or finely chopped garlic clove.

Flatbreads
200 g (7 oz) **self-raising flour**
1 teaspoon **baking powder**
1 teaspoon **cumin seeds**, roughly crushed
2 tablespoons chopped fresh **mint**
salt and freshly ground **black pepper**
2 tablespoons **olive oil**

Place the flour, baking powder, cumin seeds, mint and a little seasoning in a bowl. Add the olive oil and gradually mix in 6–7 tablespoons of water to create a soft but not sticky dough. Lightly knead and cut into four pieces.

Preheat a large ridged frying pan. While it heats up, roll each piece of dough out on a lightly floured surface to an oval about the size of your hand. As soon as the pan is hot, add as many breads as you can fit on it and cook for 3 minutes on each side or until the bread is puffy and browned with grill lines.

Spinach & Stilton tarts

These dainty individual tarts are a great addition to any picnic or make a tasty change for a packed lunch.

Makes 12
Preparation time:
  25 minutes +
  30 minutes chilling +
  cooling
Cooking time:
  20 minutes

Pastry
125 g (4½ oz) **wholewheat flour**
125 g (4½ oz) **plain flour**
a pinch of **salt**
60 g (2¼ oz) **butter**, diced
60 g (2¼ oz) **white vegetable fat**, diced

Filling
200 g (7 oz) **spinach**, washed and large stalks discarded
125 g (4½ oz) **smoked streaky bacon**, diced
4 eggs
150 ml (5 fl oz) **milk**
125 g (4½ oz) **Stilton**, diced
salt and freshly ground **black pepper**

To make the pastry, put the flours and salt into a bowl, add the fats and rub in with your fingertips or use an electric mixer until you get fine crumbs. Gradually mix in about 3 tablespoons of cold water to make a smooth dough, mixing at first with a round-bladed knife or electric mixer and then squeezing together with your hands.

Knead the dough lightly and then roll out thinly (to about 3 mm/⅛ inch) on a lightly floured surface. Stamp out 12 x 10 cm (4 inch) rounds with a plain biscuit cutter. Press into sections of a deep muffin tin, rerolling the pastry as needed until all 12 sections are lined. Chill for 30 minutes.

Preheat the oven to 190°C/375°F/Gas Mark 5. Heat a non-stick frying pan, add the spinach and dry fry for 2–3 minutes, stirring until just wilted. Transfer to a sieve, press out any liquid and then finely chop.

Drain the frying pan of water if needed and dry fry the bacon, stirring until crisp and golden.

Beat the eggs and milk together with a little seasoning. Mix in the spinach and then divide the mixture between the tart cases. Sprinkle over the bacon and Stilton and bake for about 20 minutes until the filling is set and golden.

Leave to cool for 10 minutes and then loosen the edges of the tarts with a round-bladed knife and lift out of the tin. Serve warm or leave to cool completely.

Variations
Spinach has been used here, but the tops of rainbow or plain green chard could also be used.

For a vegetarian version, omit the bacon and double check that the cheese carries the vegetarian approved symbol.

Indonesian fried rice

This is a great recipe to use up small amounts of home-grown veggies that aren't really enough to do anything with on their own.

Serves 4
**Preparation and
   cooking time:
   30 minutes**

200 g (7 oz) **basmati rice**
4 **eggs**
salt and freshly ground
   black pepper
2 tablespoons **sunflower oil**
1 **onion**, thinly sliced
150 g (5½ oz) **carrots**, cut
   into thin sticks
115 g (4¼ oz) **French beans**,
   halved
200 g (7 oz) rainbow or
   ordinary **chard** or **pak
   choi**, stems cut into thin
   sticks, leaves thickly
   sliced
2 **garlic cloves**, sliced
2.5 cm (1 inch) fresh **root
   ginger**, peeled and finely
   chopped
2 tablespoons **soy sauce**
2 teaspoons **fish sauce**
85 g (3 oz) **salted peanuts**
a small bunch of fresh
   coriander or **basil**, torn
   (optional)

Put the rice into a sieve, rinse well with cold water and drain. Pour 600 ml (20 fl oz) of water into a large lidded saucepan, bring to the boil and add the rice. Bring the water back to the boil, cover and simmer for 8 minutes. Turn off the heat and leave to stand, covered, for 5 minutes. Drain.

Meanwhile, beat the eggs with a little seasoning in a bowl. Heat ½ tablespoon of the oil in a large frying pan, add the eggs and cook for a few minutes until you have a thin omelette. Roll up tightly, slide out of the pan and set aside.

Add a little more oil to the pan, add the onion, carrots and beans and stir fry for 3 minutes until just tender. Add the chard or pak choi with the garlic and ginger and cook for 2 minutes until the leaves have just wilted.

Add the drained rice, cook for another 2 minutes until hot and then add the soy sauce, fish sauce and peanuts. Thinly slice the omelette and sprinkle over the top. Garnish with the torn herbs, if using, and serve immediately.

Variation If you have a little cold cooked chicken or ham, this can be cut into thin shreds and added along with the rice.

Spinach & fish pancakes

Adding just-cooked spinach to pancakes may not seem an obvious choice, but it makes them the most amazingly vibrant colour.

Serves 4
**Preparation and
   cooking time:
   45 minutes**

100 g (3½ oz) **plain flour**
salt
2 **eggs**
1 tablespoon **sunflower oil**,
   plus extra for frying
250 ml (9 fl oz) **milk**
450 g (1 lb) **smoked haddock**
400 g (14 oz) **spinach**,
   washed and large stalks
   discarded
250 g (9 oz) **mascarpone
   cheese**
a little grated **nutmeg**
freshly ground **black pepper**
4 tablespoons freshly grated
   Parmesan cheese

First make the pancake batter. Place the flour and a pinch of salt in a liquidiser or food processor, add the eggs and 1 tablespoon of oil, gradually pour in the milk and blend until smooth. Set aside, leaving the batter in the liquidiser or food processor.

Put the fish on a plate, cutting it into two or three pieces if it is one large fillet. Cover with cling film, pierce and cook in the microwave on high for 3½–4 minutes until cooked and the fish flakes easily when pressed with a knife. (You may need to move the pieces around on the plate halfway through cooking so that it cooks evenly in the centre.)

Heat a saucepan, add the spinach and cook for 2–3 minutes until just wilted. Drain off any water. Add one-third of the spinach to the pancake batter in the liquidiser or food processor and blitz until finely chopped. Add the mascarpone, nutmeg and a little seasoning to the remaining spinach in the pan. Heat gently, stirring until the mascarpone has melted.

Flake the fish into pieces, discarding any bones and skin, and add the flakes and any fishy cooking juices to the warm pan of spinach.

Heat a little oil in a 20 cm (8 inch) frying pan, pour out the excess and reserve in a small bowl, and then pour a little pancake batter into the pan, tilting the pan and swirling the batter into a thin layer that covers the base of the pan. Cook for 2 minutes or until golden on the underside. Loosen with a palette knife, turn over and cook the second side. Remove from the pan and keep hot. Continue until all the pancake batter has been cooked and you have eight pancakes.

Divide the warm fish mixture between the pancakes, roll up and sprinkle with the Parmesan. Serve at once.

Salmon & rocket fettuccine

The idea of making your own pesto may seem fiddly, but if you have a food processor or liquidiser it can be blitzed together in just a matter of minutes.

Serves 4
Preparation time:
  10 minutes
Cooking time:
  10 minutes

salt and freshly ground
  black pepper
400 g (14 oz) dried
  fettuccine, linguine or
  spaghetti
4 × 125 g (4½ oz) **salmon**
  fillets
juice of 1 **lemon**

Pesto
50 g (1¾ oz) **rocket**, plus
  extra to serve
65 g (2½ oz) **Parmesan**
  cheese, roughly chopped
3 tablespoons **pine nuts**
120 ml (4 fl oz) **olive oil**

To serve
rocket
grated **Parmesan cheese**

First make the pesto by placing the rocket, Parmesan and pine nuts in a food processor or liquidiser. Add a little seasoning and a splash of oil and blitz until roughly chopped. Gradually trickle in the remaining oil with the motor running until a coarse paste forms.

Fill the base of a steamer with water, bring to the boil and then add the pasta. Arrange the salmon in the steamer top, cover and steam for 8 minutes until the salmon flakes when just pressed with a knife and the pasta is tender with a little bite. If your steamer isn't very large, cook the pasta in a separate pan or adjust the steamer lid so that some of the steam can escape and the pasta water doesn't boil over.

Drain the pasta, return to the empty pan and stir in the pesto. Flake the salmon into pieces, discarding any skin and bones, and toss with the lemon juice and a little seasoning. Add to the pasta and gently toss together. Heat through if needed. Spoon into bowls and garnish the top of each with a few extra rocket leaves and a little grated Parmesan. Serve immediately.

Tips This is delicious served as it is, or you might also like to add a few fresh peas, tiny mange tout or sliced runner beans with the salmon as it steams.

Traditionally made with basil leaves, rocket adds a slightly peppery taste to the pesto and it is a great way of using up those larger less attractive leaves. If you don't have quite enough leaves, make up the quantity with basil leaves, parsley or chives, or try it with mizuna instead.

Summer roast chicken

Add a little extra zing to a Sunday roast by spooning a finely chopped herb, butter and lemon mixture under the skin of the bird before roasting.

Serves 4
Preparation and cooking time: 2 hours

1.5 kg (3 lb 5 oz) whole **chicken**
2 tablespoons **olive oil**
4 rashers **smoked streaky bacon**
500 g (1 lb 2 oz) baby **new potatoes**, scrubbed
150 g (5½ oz) mixed **beans**
150 g (5½ oz) **asparagus spears** or **peas**

Herb butter
25 g (1 oz) mixed fresh **basil** and **parsley**, finely chopped
3 teaspoons **capers**, drained and chopped
2 teaspoons **Dijon mustard**
85 g (3 oz) **butter**, softened
grated zest and juice of 1 **lemon**, squeezed lemon halves reserved
salt and freshly ground **black pepper**

Preheat the oven to 190°C/375°F/Gas Mark 5. To make the herb butter, place the herbs, capers and mustard in a bowl and beat in the butter. Add the lemon zest and mix in the lemon juice and a little seasoning.

Insert a small sharp knife between the skin and the flesh at the top of one of the chicken breasts and enlarge to make a small slit. Slide a finger into the slit and gently move the finger under the skin until it is loosened all over the breast and makes a pocket for the herb butter. Repeat on the second breast, being careful not to tear the skin.

Using a teaspoon, spoon half the herb butter under the chicken skin and then ease over both breasts to make a thin even layer of herb butter. Transfer the chicken to a roasting tin and place the squeezed lemon halves in the body cavity. Drizzle the oil over the chicken breast and legs, cover the breast with the bacon and loosely cover with foil. Roast for 50 minutes.

Baste the chicken and cover again with foil. Add the new potatoes to the base of the tin and turn in the juices, but do not cover these with foil. Roast for 20 minutes, remove the foil from the chicken and baste. Turn the potatoes

and baste these too. Return to the oven and roast for 20 minutes or until the chicken is cooked through. To test, insert a skewer through the thickest part of the leg; if the juices run clear the chicken is ready. Turn off the oven and keep the chicken and potatoes hot.

When the chicken is almost ready, add the beans to a saucepan of boiling water and cook for 3–6 minutes until almost tender. Add the asparagus or peas and cook for 3–4 minutes until just tender. Drain, toss with the remaining herb butter and add to the potatoes. Carve the chicken and serve.

Tip For gravy fans, transfer the chicken and vegetables to a serving plate. Pour off nearly all the fat from the roasting tin and add 450 ml (16 fl oz) of chicken stock and a little white wine to the pan juices. Boil rapidly for a few minutes, stirring and scraping up the bits from the base of the tin. Strain and serve with the carved chicken and vegetables.

Variation It can also be nice to add the chopped herbs to a cream cheese base rather than butter and flavour it with a few chopped pistachio nuts and a little garlic.

Sausage & bean supper

Make this with fresh beans from the garden in one large frying pan for an easy midweek supper. Serve with crusty bread or hot garlic bread.

Serves 4
Preparation time:
  15 minutes
Cooking time:
  20 minutes

1 tablespoon **sunflower oil**
12 **Cumberland chipolata sausages**
1 **onion**, chopped
½ teaspoon **smoked** or ordinary **paprika**
300 g (10½ oz) podded **broad beans**
225 g (8 oz) **cherry tomatoes**, halved, or larger **tomatoes**, roughly chopped
300 ml (10 fl oz) **chicken stock**
1 tablespoon **tomato purée**
salt and freshly ground **black pepper**
115 g (4¼ oz) **runner beans**, thinly shredded

Heat the oil in a large frying pan, add the sausages and fry for 5 minutes, until browned on one side. Turn the sausages, draining off any excess fat to leave about 1 tablespoon, add the onion and fry for another 5 minutes, turning the sausages occasionally until brown all over and the onions are golden.

Stir in the paprika, broad beans and tomatoes. Pour in the stock, add the tomato purée and some seasoning and simmer for 5 minutes.

Add the runner beans and simmer for another 5 minutes until the sausages are cooked through and the sauce reduced slightly.

Spoon into shallow soup bowls and serve.

Variations Try this with gourmet spiced sausages too – thin merguez sausages would taste delicious but can be difficult to find. If you use larger sausages then fry for longer before adding the onions.

You can use borlotti beans instead of broad beans if you like.

Four ways with cabbage

Spring greens with chilli & anchovy
Serves 4
Preparation and cooking time: 10–15 minutes

25 g (1 oz) **butter**
1 tablespoon **olive oil**
1 small **onion**, finely chopped
300 g (10½ oz) **spring cabbage**, thickly sliced
a large pinch of **chilli flakes**
4 **anchovies**, chopped
salt and freshly ground **black pepper**

Heat the butter and oil in a large lidded frying pan, add the onion and fry until softened. Add the cabbage, chilli flakes, anchovies and seasoning. Cover and cook over a gentle heat for 5–8 minutes, stirring from time to time until softened.

Colcannon
Serves 4
Preparation and cooking time: 30 minutes

650 g (1 lb 7 oz) **potatoes**, peeled and cut into chunks
225 g (8 oz) **Savoy cabbage**, thinly sliced
1 small **leek**, thinly sliced
55 g (2 oz) **butter**
4–6 tablespoons **milk**
a little grated **nutmeg**
salt and freshly ground **black pepper**

Bring a saucepan of water to the boil, add the potatoes and cook for about 15 minutes until almost tender. Steam the cabbage and leek above the potatoes for 4–5 minutes until just tender. Drain the potatoes well, add the butter and half the milk and mash until smooth. Stir in the cabbage, leek, nutmeg and seasoning. Beat in extra milk, as needed, to make a soft mash.

Curly kale with sesame seeds
Serves 4
Preparation and cooking time: 10–15 minutes

1 tablespoon **sunflower oil**
3 tablespoons **sesame seeds**
300 g (10½ oz) **curly kale** or **Savoy cabbage**, thickly sliced
2.5 cm (1 inch) fresh **root ginger**, peeled and finely chopped
2 tablespoons **soy sauce**

Heat the oil in a large lidded frying pan, add the sesame seeds and fry for 2–3 minutes until lightly toasted. Add the kale or cabbage with the ginger, quickly cover and cook for 3–4 minutes, shaking the pan from time to time until just tender. Add the soy sauce, cook uncovered for 1–2 minutes, stirring until the leaves are tender.

Savoy cabbage with bacon & almonds
Serves 4
Preparation and cooking time: 20 minutes

300 g (10½ oz) **Savoy cabbage**, thinly sliced
1 tablespoon **sunflower oil**
15 g (½ oz) **flaked almonds**
4 rashers **smoked streaky bacon**, diced
salt and freshly ground **black pepper**
25 g (1 oz) **butter**

Add the cabbage leaves to a saucepan of boiling water and cook for 2 minutes. Drain, rinse with cold water and drain again. Heat the oil in a frying pan, add the almonds and fry, stirring until golden. Scoop out of the pan and reserve. Add the bacon and fry, stirring for 4–5 minutes until golden. Add the cabbage and seasoning and fry for 2–3 minutes until piping hot. Add the butter, stir until melted and then sprinkle with the almonds.

Salmon & saffron parcels

You can prepare these parcels in advance, leave in the fridge and just pop in the oven when you're ready. Serve with crusty bread.

Serves 4
Preparation time:
  15 minutes
Cooking time:
  20–25 minutes

175 g (6 oz) **French beans**, halved or cut into three
200 g (7 oz) **courgettes**, sliced
250 g (9 oz) **tomatoes**, roughly chopped
4 **spring onions**, sliced
salt and freshly ground **black pepper**
4 × 150 g (5½ oz) **salmon fillets**
2 large pinches of **saffron**
4 teaspoons **boiling water**
4 tablespoons **white wine** or **fish stock**
a small bunch of fresh **basil**

Preheat the oven to 180°C/350°F/Gas Mark 4. Tear four large pieces of non-stick baking parchment off a roll and spread out on the work surface. (Or use four plastic roasting bags if preferred.)

Add the beans to a saucepan of boiling water and blanch for 1–2 minutes until almost tender. Drain, rinse with cold water and drain again.

Divide the beans, courgettes, tomatoes and spring onions between the pieces of paper. Season, arrange the pieces of salmon on top and season again.

Mix the saffron with the boiling water and leave to stand for a few minutes before drizzling over the salmon. Add a spoonful of wine or stock and a few torn basil leaves to each parcel and then bring the edges of the paper up and over the salmon. Fold and twist together a few times and then fold and twist the sides together to make a well-sealed parcel. Chill at this stage if cooking at a later time.

Put the parcels in a roasting tin and bake for 20–25 minutes. To test if they are ready, open one of the parcels and press a knife into the centre of the salmon. If it breaks easily into flakes that are pale pink, and if the beans are tender, then the parcels are ready to serve. Transfer to serving plates and allow diners to open the parcels themselves.

Tip If you don't have any saffron then add a little grated lemon zest instead.

Broad bean bruschetta

This is rather like posh beans on toast, but lifted to a gourmet level by topping with a lightly poached egg and a little grated black truffle.

Serves 4
Preparation time:
  20 minutes
Cooking time:
  10–12 minutes

4–5 tablespoons **olive oil**
6 **spring onions**, sliced
2 **garlic cloves**, finely
  chopped
300 g (10½ oz) podded
  broad beans
200 ml (7 fl oz) **vegetable**
  or **chicken stock**
salt and freshly ground
  black pepper
a small bunch of fresh
  chives, roughly chopped
8 slices **French** or **ciabatta**
  bread
1 teaspoon **white wine**
  vinegar
4 **eggs**
a little grated **black truffle**
  (optional)

Heat 2 tablespoons of oil in a frying pan, add the spring onions and fry for 2–3 minutes until just softened. Add the garlic, broad beans, stock and a generous sprinkling of seasoning. Simmer for 5 minutes until the broad beans are just tender.

Mash the beans until you get a coarse purée or blitz in a food processor or liquidiser. Stir in half the chives. Keep hot in a bowl.

Brush one side of each slice of bread with a little oil and toast in a ridged frying pan until golden. Brush the second side with a little more oil, turn over and toast until golden.

Meanwhile, bring a medium-sized saucepan of water to the boil. Add the vinegar and a little salt. Break an egg into a cup and then slide the egg into the gently simmering water. Repeat with the remaining eggs. Cook for 3–4 minutes until the whites are set and the yolks still runny, or until done to your preference.

Spread the mashed beans over the hot toasts and divide between four serving plates. Drain the eggs well and add one to each plate. Sprinkle with a little extra seasoning, the remaining chives and a little finely grated truffle, if using. Serve immediately.

Tips If you don't have quite enough broad beans, make up the weight with podded peas or simply halve the recipe and serve two.

Truffles are available in small jars and a little does go a long way, but this is very much an optional extra.

Variation You might also like to spread the broad bean pâté on to smaller bread croûtes and top with some green olives, a little torn mozzarella and some chopped herbs. Serve with a chilled glass of white wine, instead of a starter, when friends come for supper.

Green bean risotto

Risotto is one of those dishes that is infinitely flexible; green beans have been added here, but the choice of vegetable is very much up to you.

**Serves 4
Preparation and
 cooking time:
 40 minutes**

2 tablespoons **olive oil**
150 g (5½ oz) **fennel**, chopped
225 g (8 oz) **risotto rice**
1.2–1.3 litres (2–2¼ pints)
 vegetable stock
200 ml (7 fl oz) **dry white wine**
salt and freshly ground **black
 pepper**
115 g (4¼ oz) **French beans**,
 halved
50 g (1¾ oz) **mange tout**,
 halved
55 g (2 oz) **Parmesan cheese**,
 grated, plus extra to serve

Herb butter
70 g (2½ oz) **butter**
1 tablespoon chopped **fennel
 fronds**
2 tablespoons chopped fresh
 chives
2 **garlic cloves**, finely
 chopped
¼ teaspoon roughly crushed
 black peppercorns

First make the herb butter by beating all the ingredients together. Spoon on to a piece of greaseproof or non-stick baking parchment, shape into a roll and chill in the fridge while making the risotto.

Heat the oil in a large non-stick frying pan, add the fennel and fry for 5 minutes until softened and only just beginning to colour around the edges. Add the rice and stir.

Bring the stock to the boil in a saucepan. Stir the wine and a generous sprinkling of seasoning into the rice and then add a ladleful of hot stock. Simmer for about 20 minutes, stirring from time to time and topping up with ladlefuls of stock, as needed, until the rice is tender and nearly all the stock has been absorbed.

When the rice is almost cooked, about 5 minutes or so from the end of cooking, add the beans. When they are almost cooked add the mange tout, cook for 2 minutes and then stir in the Parmesan and one-third of the herb butter, until melted.

Spoon into shallow soup bowls and top with slices of herb butter and extra Parmesan. Garnish with extra fennel fronds if liked.

Variations If you are not serving veggie diners, you might like to top the risotto with some crispy fried Parma ham or streaky bacon, cut into strips.

Diced beetroot, pumpkin or courgettes can also be added, or, if you are lucky enough to have some asparagus, then add some trimmed and halved spears along with the beans.

If you don't like fennel, replace it with leeks or onions and replace the fennel fronds with fresh sage.

Steak & chermoula salad

Salads needn't include lettuce, as this hearty man-sized one proves.
The dressing doubles as a marinade.

Serves 4
Preparation and
cooking time:
   40 minutes +
   30 minutes marinating

1 teaspoon **cumin seeds**,
   roughly crushed
½ teaspoon **allspice berries**,
   roughly crushed
2 teaspoons **light muscovado**
   sugar
4 tablespoons **olive oil**
grated zest and juice of
   1 **lemon**
salt
cayenne pepper
4 **lamb rump steaks**
500 g (1 lb 2 oz) baby **new**
   potatoes, scrubbed and
   thickly sliced
225 g (8 oz) mixed **green**
   beans, dwarf beans,
   thickly sliced, and **runner**
   beans, thinly shredded
1 small **red onion**, thinly sliced
edible **flower petals**,
   sprouting radish seeds or
   fresh **parsley**, to garnish

Mix the crushed cumin seeds and allspice berries with the sugar, oil, lemon zest and juice and a generous sprinkling of salt and cayenne pepper. Put the steaks in a single layer in a non-metallic dish and pour over a generous third of the dressing, reserving the remainder. Leave to marinate for 30 minutes.

Add the potatoes to a saucepan of boiling water and cook for 15 minutes. Add all the beans to the pan and cook for another 4–5 minutes until just tender.

Meanwhile, preheat a non-stick frying pan. Lift the steaks out of the marinade, reserving the marinade, add the steaks to the pan and fry for 10 minutes, turning once, until browned on the outside and with just a hint of pink in the centre. Set aside.

Drain the vegetables and place in a large shallow dish. Stir the reserved dressing together once more, add to the vegetables with the onion and toss together.

Add the reserved marinade to the frying pan, cook for 1 minute and then pour over the salad. Adjust the seasoning if needed.

Thinly slice the steaks and arrange on top of the salad. Garnish with edible flower petals, sprouting radish seeds or chopped parsley. Serve while hot.

Tips If you don't have a pestle and mortar to crush the cumin and allspice, then improvise and use a mug and the end of a rolling pin, or use ready ground spices if you would prefer.

Beans need a lot of water to grow. To help keep moisture in the soil, dig a deep trench before planting the seedlings, add a thick layer of old newspapers, water, cover with a thin layer of soil, repeat, plant and then fill the trench back up with soil.

Variation This recipe also works well with beef steaks, just reduce the cooking time so that the steak is done just the way you like it.

Portuguese green soup

This rustic peasant style soup is really a main course in a bowl. Serve with warm bread.

Serves 4
Preparation time:
10 minutes
Cooking time:
40 minutes

2 tablespoons **olive oil**
2 **onions**, roughly chopped
115 g (4¼ oz) **chorizo sausage**, diced
450 g (1 lb) **potatoes**, peeled and cubed
1 litre (1¾ pints) **chicken stock**
2 fresh **rosemary** sprigs
salt and freshly ground **black pepper**
150 g (5½ oz) **spring greens** or **Savoy cabbage**, shredded

Heat the oil in a medium-sized lidded saucepan, add the onions and chorizo and fry gently for 10 minutes, stirring from time to time until the onion is just beginning to turn golden. Add the potatoes and cook for 5 minutes, stirring more frequently, until just beginning to soften.

Pour in the stock, tear the rosemary leaves from the stems into the soup and season generously. Bring to the boil, cover and simmer for 20 minutes until the vegetables are tender.

Add the spring greens or cabbage to the soup and cook for 5 minutes until just softened but still bright green. Ladle into shallow bowls.

Tip There are so many different varieties of cabbage to choose from that, with a little planning, it is possible to grow cabbage all year round.

Fragrant noodle broth

This oriental-style clear broth mixed with fine noodles provides a good base for whatever vegetables you have growing in the garden.

Serves 4
Preparation and cooking time: 25 minutes

1 tablespoon **sunflower oil**
1 **onion**, finely chopped
1 **garlic clove**, finely chopped
2.5 cm (1 inch) fresh **root ginger**, peeled and finely chopped
1–2 teaspoons **green Thai curry paste**
1 litre (1¾ pints) **chicken** or **vegetable stock**
1 tablespoon **soy sauce**
2 teaspoons **caster sugar**
200 g (7 oz) **purple sprouting broccoli**, stems cut into 4 cm (1½ inch) lengths
115 g (4¼ oz) **rainbow chard**, stems cut into 4 cm (1½ inch) lengths and tops thickly sliced, or **spring cabbage**, thickly sliced
150 g (5½ oz) **straight-to-wok fine noodles**
a small bunch of fresh **basil**, **coriander** or **mint**, torn (optional)

Heat the oil in a saucepan, add the onion, garlic and ginger and fry gently for 2–3 minutes, stirring until softened.

Stir in the curry paste, cook for a few seconds and then pour in the stock. Add the soy sauce and sugar, bring to the boil and simmer for 5 minutes.

Add the broccoli and cook for 5 minutes until almost tender. Add the chard stems and leaves or cabbage and cook for 2 minutes until all the vegetables are just cooked.

Add the noodles, cook for 1 minute until hot and then ladle into bowls. Sprinkle with the torn herbs, if using.

Tip Chard is one of those good value vegetables that is easy to grow, produces a bountiful crop and, if you are lucky, will keep going throughout the year. Although white stemmed varieties may be hardier, the multi-coloured stem varieties that range from yellow to deep pink are worth growing for their looks alone.

Runner bean salad

To make this into a main meal salad you may like to add some tuna fish, Feta cheese, chorizo or grilled mackerel. Serve with warm crusty bread.

Serves 4
Preparation time:
  15 minutes
Cooking time:
  1–2 minutes

225 g (8 oz) **runner beans**,
  thinly sliced
225 g (8 oz) **tomatoes**, diced
1 **red onion**, halved and
  thinly sliced
a small bunch of fresh
  parsley, roughly chopped
1 **Little Gem lettuce**, leaves
  separated, or a handful of
  mixed salad leaves

Dressing
3 tablespoons **olive oil**
1 tablespoon **red wine**
  vinegar
2 teaspoons **harissa paste**
½ teaspoon **caster sugar**
1 **garlic clove**, finely
  chopped
salt and freshly ground
  black pepper

Bring a medium-sized saucepan of water to the boil, add the runner beans and cook for 1–2 minutes, depending on the size and age of the beans. Drain, rinse with cold water and drain again.

Add the beans to a large salad bowl with the tomatoes, onion and parsley.

Put all the dressing ingredients in a screw-topped jam jar, add the lid and shake. Pour over the salad and toss together gently. Tear the salad leaves into bite-sized pieces and gently toss with the salad.

Tips Runner beans are perhaps the most prolific of all the beans; nearly every flower will become a bean, but they do need to be picked on an almost daily basis. Try to pick the beans when they are about 18 cm (7 inches) long, flat and about the width of a finger. By the time the beans are 23 cm (9 inches) long they will need to have the side strings removed, but if they are still flat they will still be tender although may need a minute or two longer in cooking. Once the beans begin to bulge with large seeds they will taste very fibrous and tough. Try to pick the beans while still young and store in the chiller drawer in the fridge for up to a week, rather than leave them growing outside to become bigger and woodier.

If you haven't used harissa before, it is rather like the Moroccan version of a hot spicy pesto, made with oil, chilli, garlic, lemon, caraway and coriander. It is sold in small jars alongside the other spices in the supermarket or in the ethnic foods section.

Lamb daube & vegetables

Slow cook budget-priced neck of lamb for a wonderfully comforting supper dish that could be shared with friends.

Serves 4
Preparation and cooking time: 3 hours

2 tablespoons **olive oil**
900 g (2 lb) **neck of lamb**
350 g (12 oz) **shallots**
2 **garlic cloves**, finely chopped (optional)
2 tablespoons **plain flour**
450 ml (16 fl oz) **lamb stock**
200 ml (7 fl oz) **red wine**
1 tablespoon **redcurrant jelly**
salt and freshly ground **black pepper**
500 g (1 lb 2 oz) new or baking **potatoes**
3 fresh **rosemary sprigs**

To finish
175 g (6 oz) **baby carrots**
150 g (5½ oz) young **runner beans**, sliced
115 g (4¼ oz) podded **broad beans** or **asparagus**
a small bunch of fresh **mint**, roughly chopped (optional)

Preheat the oven to 160°C/325°F/Gas Mark 3. Heat the oil in a large frying pan, add the lamb and brown on both sides. Lift out of the pan with a slotted spoon and transfer to a large, lidded, ovenproof casserole dish.

Halve the shallots if large, add to the frying pan and fry for 4–5 minutes until just beginning to brown. Stir in the garlic, if using, cook briefly, sprinkle over the flour and stir to mix. Pour in the stock and wine, add the redcurrant jelly and plenty of seasoning and bring to the boil, stirring.

Scrub the potatoes and cut into chunks if they are large. Add to the casserole dish with the rosemary and then pour over the hot stock mixture. Cover with the lid and cook in the oven for 2½ hours until the lamb is very tender.

Meanwhile, scrub the carrots and halve lengthways depending on their size.

When the lamb is almost ready, half fill the base of a steamer with water, bring to the boil, add the carrots to the top of the steamer and cook for 5 minutes. Add the runner beans and broad beans and steam for 7–10 minutes. If using asparagus, add for the last 5 minutes of cooking.

Stir the lamb, ladle into shallow soup bowls, add the steamed vegetables and then ladle over a generous spoonful of the sauce. Sprinkle with the chopped mint and serve immediately.

Tip If you have some baby turnips or beetroot you may also like to steam these too, or perhaps add some mange tout or baby pea pods for the last few minutes. Small lamb shanks, lamb chump chops or a half a shoulder of lamb can also be cooked this way.

Roast pork with vegetables

You just need one pan for this rustic style roast as all the vegetables are added to the joint towards the end of cooking.

Serves 6
Preparation time:
  30 minutes
Cooking time: 2 hours
  30–40 minutes

2 **onions**, thickly sliced
6–8 fresh **thyme sprigs**,
  depending on size
1.75 kg (4 lb) boned thick
  end of **belly pork**, rind
  scored
a little **olive oil**
salt
750 g (1 lb 10 oz) **new
  potatoes**, scrubbed and
  large ones halved
700 g (1 lb 9 oz) **courgettes**,
  thickly sliced
2 different coloured
  peppers, halved,
  de-seeded and cut into
  large chunks
350 g (12 oz) **tomatoes**,
  halved
4 **garlic cloves**, halved
freshly ground **black pepper**
150 ml (5 fl oz) **red** or **white
  wine**

Preheat the oven to 180°C/350°F/Gas Mark 4. Place the onions in a roasting tin, arranged in a mound about the same size as the pork joint. Lay half the thyme sprigs on top and put the pork joint on top of that. Rub a little oil and salt into the rind and roast, uncovered, for 1¾ hours, spooning the pan juices over halfway through cooking.

Pour off most of the fat from the roasting tin to leave about 3 tablespoons. Reserve the drained fat in case you need it later. Add the potatoes to the tin and toss them in the pan juices. Roast for 15 minutes and then take the tin out of the oven. Increase the oven temperature to 200°C/400°F/Gas Mark 6.

Turn the potatoes, add all the remaining vegetables and thyme with the garlic, sprinkle the vegetables with a little seasoning and toss them in the pan juices. If there aren't quite enough juices to coat, drizzle over a little of the fat that you drained off earlier.

Roast for 30–40 minutes until the vegetables are tender and the potatoes are browned. Insert a small sharp knife into the centre of the pork – if the juices run clear the pork is ready. If the pork rind hasn't crackled sufficiently, transfer the pork to the base of the grill pan

and cook under the grill for a few minutes until the top is crisp, but keep a watchful eye so that it doesn't catch.

Transfer the pork to a serving dish and the vegetables to a second dish. Add the wine to the roasting tin and heat the tin on the hob until the pan juices are bubbling. Pour into a jug.

Carve the pork into thick slices (you may find it easier to remove the crackling first and snip this into pieces with kitchen scissors). Serve with the vegetables and sauce.

Tips Vary the vegetables depending on what you have in the garden; thickly sliced squash or chunky pieces of aubergine also work well.

Score the pork rind with a new craft or Stanley knife and keep it especially for this purpose. You will find it much easier to use than a kitchen knife.

Allotment curry

Inspired by retro 1950s egg curries, this quick and easy curry has a mild aromatic flavour. Serve with rice and warmed naan breads.

Serves 4
Preparation and
cooking time:
1 hour

1 tablespoon **sunflower oil**
1 **onion**, roughly chopped
1 teaspoon **coriander seeds**
1 teaspoon **cumin seeds**
2 **garlic cloves**
1 teaspoon **turmeric**
1 teaspoon **garam masala**
½ teaspoon **chilli flakes**
300 g (10½ oz) peeled and
   de-seeded **pumpkin**
450 g (1 lb) **tomatoes**,
   roughly chopped
400 g can **lentils**, drained
300 ml (10 fl oz) **vegetable**
   stock
1 teaspoon **caster sugar**
salt and freshly ground
   black pepper
115 g (4¼ oz) **runner beans**
175 g (6 oz) podded **peas**
   and **broad beans**
6 **eggs**
150 ml (5 fl oz) **double cream**
a small bunch of fresh **mint**
   or **coriander**, chopped

Heat the oil in a large lidded saucepan, add the onion and fry for 5 minutes, stirring from time to time until softened and just beginning to brown around the edges. Crush the coriander and cumin seeds and finely chop the garlic. Add to the pan with the turmeric, garam masala and chilli flakes, stir and cook for a few seconds. Cut the pumpkin into cubes and add with the tomatoes.

Add the lentils, stock, sugar and plenty of seasoning and then cover and simmer for 20 minutes, stirring occasionally until the pumpkin is almost tender. Meanwhile, shred the runner beans.

Stir in the green vegetables, cover and cook for 10 minutes.

Meanwhile, add the eggs to a second pan, cover with cold water, bring just to the boil and simmer for 8 minutes. Drain, rinse with cold water, crack the shells and, when cool enough to handle, peel off the shells. Halve the eggs.

Stir the cream and half the herbs into the curry, arrange the eggs on top, cover and heat through. Spoon on to plates, sprinkle with the remaining herbs and serve.

Tip If you don't have any fresh tomatoes in the garden then cheat and use a 400 g can of chopped tomatoes instead. Mix and match the types of green vegetables depending on what you have in the garden, and aim for a total of 280 g (10 oz). If using spinach or chard, add this for the last 3–4 minutes of cooking.

Variation You could also add some cold leftover chicken from a roast or a handful of prawns.

Freeform tomato tarts

If you find that your tomatoes all seem to be ripening at the same time, transform them into a summery main course. Serve with a green salad.

Serves 4
Preparation time:
  20 minutes
Cooking time:
  50 minutes

2 tablespoons **olive oil**
1 **onion**, chopped
2 **garlic cloves**, finely
  chopped
450 g (1 lb) **tomatoes**,
  skinned (optional) and
  roughly chopped
1 teaspoon **caster sugar**
1 teaspoon **balsamic
  vinegar**
1 tablespoon **sun-dried
  tomato purée**
4 fresh **basil sprigs**, torn,
  plus extra to garnish
salt and freshly ground
  black pepper
500 g (1 lb 2 oz) frozen **puff
  pastry**, defrosted
450 g (1 lb) small mixed
  heritage tomatoes, sliced
25 g (1 oz) **Parmesan
  cheese**

Preheat the oven to 200°C/400°F/Gas Mark 6.

To make the tomato sauce, heat 1 tablespoon of oil in a saucepan, add the onion and fry for 5 minutes until softened and just beginning to brown around the edges. Add the garlic and tomatoes, fry for a minute or two and then stir in the sugar, vinegar and tomato purée. Add the basil leaves, season generously and cook over a medium heat for 15 minutes until you have a thick pulpy sauce. Stir more frequently towards the end of cooking to prevent the sauce from sticking to the pan.

Cut the pastry in half, roll each half out on a lightly floured surface and trim to a 25 × 18 cm (10 × 7 inch) rectangle. Transfer to a lightly oiled large baking tray and score 2.5 cm (1 inch) in from the edge of the pastry. Be careful not to cut through to the base. Prick the inner rectangle with a fork.

Bake the pastry for 10 minutes until it is well risen and partly cooked. Take the baking tray out of the oven and press the centre of the pastry down with the back of a fork, inside the marked line, to make a deep tart case.

Spoon half the tomato sauce into each tart in an even layer, arrange the sliced heritage tomatoes on top and season generously. Drizzle with the remaining oil and grate the Parmesan over the top.

Return to the oven and bake for 15 minutes. Serve warm, garnished with extra basil and cut into pieces.

Tip For those whose crops aren't quite so bumper, simply halve the recipe and make just one tart. Cut it into four small pieces and serve as a starter or with other dishes. This idea can also be scaled down to make tiny tarts that are just a little larger than a slice of tomato – great to serve with drinks before dinner. Make sure to reduce the cooking times down to just 5 minutes until the pastry is risen and then 5 minutes or so once the tomatoes are added.

Courgette griddle cakes

We tend to think of griddle cakes or drop scones as a teatime treat, but they are equally delicious savoury and a good way to eke out a few vegetables.

Serves 6
Preparation time:
 15 minutes
Cooking time:
 15 minutes

115 g (4¼ oz) podded **broad beans** or a mix of **broad beans** and **peas**
175 g (6 oz) **self-raising flour**
½ teaspoon **bicarbonate of soda**
salt and freshly ground **black pepper**
1 **egg**
150 g (5½ oz) **natural yogurt**
3 tablespoons **milk**
225 g (8 oz) **courgette**, coarsely grated
1 tablespoon chopped fresh **tarragon** or **chives**
2 tablespoons **sunflower oil**
a few **pea shoots**, to garnish (optional)

Add the beans or beans and peas to a saucepan of boiling water and cook for 3–4 minutes until just cooked. Drain, rinse with cold water and drain again.

Add the flour, bicarbonate of soda and a little seasoning to a mixing bowl and stir together. Add the egg, yogurt and milk, fork or whisk together until just mixed and then stir in the beans or beans and peas, courgette and herbs.

Add a little of the oil to a large non-stick frying pan, heat and then pour the excess oil into a bowl. Add large spoonfuls of the batter, well spaced apart so there is room for them to rise, and cook until bubbles begin to form and the undersides are golden. Turn them over using a palette knife and cook the second side until golden and the griddle cakes are cooked through. Transfer to a plate and keep hot, covered with a clean tea towel or napkin.

Oil the pan again and cook the rest of the batter in batches until all the mixture has been used up. Serve garnished with a few pea shoots, if liked.

Tips To make a tasty supper or light lunch, top with cream cheese and smoked salmon or cream cheese and roasted tomatoes (see below). Alternatively, spread with a little butter and top with a rasher or two of crispy bacon or good sliced ham and a poached egg.

To roast tomatoes, preheat the oven to 190°C/375°F/Gas Mark 5 and roast 450 g (1 lb) of cherry tomatoes with a drizzle of olive oil and a little seasoning for 10 minutes. Drizzle with a little balsamic vinegar to serve.

Spinach & tomato gratin

If you grow your own veg this is very much a store cupboard supper.
Serve as it is or with grilled bacon.

Serves 4
Preparation time:
20 minutes
Cooking time:
15 minutes

225 g (8 oz) **macaroni**
55 g (2 oz) **butter**
55 g (2 oz) **plain flour**
600 ml (10 fl oz) **milk**
2 teaspoons **wholegrain mustard**
225 g (8 oz) **Cheddar cheese**, grated
salt and freshly ground **black pepper**
300 g (10½ oz) **spinach**, washed and any long stems discarded
300 g (10½ oz) **tomatoes**, thickly sliced
2 teaspoons **balsamic vinegar**
25 g (1 oz) **Parmesan cheese**, finely grated
3 tablespoons fresh **breadcrumbs**

Add the pasta to a large saucepan of boiling water and simmer for 10–12 minutes until tender. Drain.

Meanwhile, melt the butter in a second slightly smaller pan, stir in the flour and cook for 1 minute. Gradually mix in the milk and bring to the boil, stirring constantly until thickened and smooth. Take off the heat and stir in the mustard, two thirds of the Cheddar and some seasoning. Stir in the macaroni.

Cook the spinach in the empty pasta pan for a minute or two until just wilted, drain off any water, roughly chop if the leaves are large and then stir into the cheese sauce. Bring back just to the boil and then tip into a shallow ovenproof dish. Preheat the grill to hot.

Arrange the sliced tomatoes on top of the mixture and drizzle with the vinegar. Mix the rest of the Cheddar with the Parmesan and breadcrumbs and sprinkle over the tomatoes.

Cook under the hot grill until the cheese is bubbling and the tomatoes are hot.

Tip There are a huge variety of tomatoes available, from tiny cherry tomatoes that grow on long trusses to large beefsteak tomatoes. This recipe is ideal for those tomatoes that are a little too ripe to add to salad.

Variation Spinach has been added to the rich cheesy sauce, but vary the vegetables depending on what you have. If using peas, broad beans or sweetcorn (taken off the cobs) add to the pasta for the last 2–3 minutes of cooking.

Pickled courgette salad

Cutting courgettes with a vegetable peeler or mandolin is a quick way of preparing them. This is a refreshing accompaniment to grilled fish.

Serves 4
Preparation time:
 10 minutes +
 15 minutes cooling
Cooking time:
 about 10 minutes

450 g (1 lb) **courgettes**
120 ml (4 fl oz) **white wine
 vinegar**
70 g (2½ oz) **caster sugar**
¼ teaspoon **chilli flakes**
2 teaspoons **coriander
 seeds**, roughly crushed
salt and freshly ground
 black pepper
4 **mackerel**, cleaned and
 heads removed
4 teaspoons **olive oil**
150 g (5½ oz) **crème fraîche**
1 teaspoon grated
 horseradish (from a jar)

To garnish
fresh **chives**, **dill** or **chervil**
chive flowers (optional)

Cut the courgettes into long thin slices with a swivel-bladed vegetable peeler or mandolin and put them into a bowl.

Put the vinegar, sugar, a large pinch of the chilli flakes and half the coriander seeds in a saucepan, season generously and bring to the boil, stirring until the sugar has dissolved. Pour over the courgettes, toss them gently in the vinegar mix and leave to cool for at least 15 minutes.

Rinse the mackerel inside and out with cold water, drain well and then slash each side two or three times with a knife and put on a piece of foil on the grill rack. Sprinkle with the remaining chilli flakes, coriander seeds and a little seasoning. Drizzle with the oil and grill for about 10 minutes, depending on the size of the fish, turning once until browned and the flesh flakes easily into pieces when pressed with a knife.

Meanwhile, mix the crème fraîche with the horseradish and a little seasoning.

To serve, transfer the mackerel to serving plates, add a spoonful of the pickled courgette salad, a spoonful of the horseradish cream and sprinkle with the herbs and chive flowers, if using.

Tips This also tastes delicious served with the Hot marinated beetroot (see page 70).

The pickled courgette salad is is best eaten fresh but will keep for 2–3 days in the fridge. The longer it is kept, the less vibrant green it will be.

Stuffed pumpkin

If you have children or grandchildren, encourage them to grow their own pumpkins. Serve with a green salad tossed with toasted walnut pieces.

Serves 4–6
Preparation and
cooking time:
1¼–1¾ hours

4 **onion** or **turban squash**
   or **pumpkins**, about
   12–15 cm (4½–6 inches)
   in diameter
1 tablespoon **olive oil**
500 g (1 lb 2 oz) **minced**
   lamb or **beef**
1 small **onion**, chopped
1 teaspoon **ground**
   cinnamon
¼ teaspoon **ground cloves**
2.5 cm (1 inch) fresh **root**
   ginger, peeled and finely
   chopped
85 g (3 oz) **long grain white**
   rice
2 teaspoons **sun-dried**
   tomato purée
2 tablespoons **currants**
2 tablespoon **pistachio nuts**,
   chopped (optional)
salt and freshly ground
   black pepper
400 ml (14 fl oz) hot **lamb** or
   chicken stock

Cut a slice off the top of the squash or pumpkins and reserve. Scoop out the seeds with a dessertspoon. Stand the squash or pumpkins in a shallow ovenproof dish or roasting tin.

Heat the oil in a frying pan, add the mince and onion and fry, stirring, for 10 minutes until the mince is browned. Mix in the spices and ginger and then the rice, tomato purée, currants and pistachio nuts, if using. Season well and spoon the mixture into the squash or pumpkins, pressing down well.

Pour the hot stock, or as much as you can fit, into the squash or pumpkins, add the tops and bake in the oven for 45 minutes–1¼ hours until the squash or pumpkins and rice are tender. Serve whole, or halved if large.

Tip For a single large squash or pumpkin (weighing 1.25–1.5 kg/2 lb 12 oz–3 lb 5 oz), bake for about 1½ hours or until tender.

Sweet spiced pumpkin pie

An all-American favourite made with roasted and puréed pumpkin in a baked spiced custard and topped with flavoured whipped cream.

Serves 6
Preparation time:
  30 minutes +
  30 minutes chilling
Cooking time: 1 hour

175 g (6 oz) **plain flour**
85 g (3 oz) **butter**, diced
40 g (1½ oz) **caster sugar**
grated zest of 1 **orange**
2 **egg yolks**

Filling
450 g (1 lb) de-seeded
  pumpkin, cut into wedges
  with the skin still on
115 g (4¼ oz) **caster sugar**
2 **eggs**
1 teaspoon **ground ginger**
½ teaspoon **ground**
  cinnamon
a pinch of **ground cloves**
1 tablespoon chopped **stem**
  or **glacé ginger**, plus
  extra to decorate

Topping
250 ml (9 fl oz) **double cream**
2 tablespoons **bourbon**
2 tablespoons **caster sugar**

Preheat the oven to 190°C/375°F/Gas Mark 5.

To make the pastry, place the flour, butter, sugar and orange zest in a bowl and rub the butter into the flour with your fingertips or an electric mixer until the mixture looks like fine crumbs. Add the egg yolks and mix with a knife and then your hands to make a smooth dough. Chill for 15 minutes.

Place the pumpkin wedges in a roasting tin with a little water in the base and roast for about 45 minutes until tender when pierced with a knife but not browned.

Meanwhile, knead the pastry very lightly, cut into six pieces and roll each piece out thinly (to about 3 mm/⅛ inch) on a floured surface until large enough to line a 9 cm (3½ inch) individual tart tin or 200 ml (7 fl oz) Yorkshire pudding tin.

Lift the pastry into the tins, trim off the excess and crimp the top edge with your fingertips or a fork. Prick the base with a fork and chill for 15 minutes.

Line the pastry cases with squares of greaseproof paper or non-stick baking parchment and baking beans and bake blind on the shelf below the pumpkin for 10 minutes.

Remove the paper and beans and cook for another 3–4 minutes until the bases are dry and crisp. Reduce the oven temperature to 180°C/350°F/Gas Mark 4.

Leave the pumpkin to cool slightly and then scoop the flesh from the skin with a spoon and add to a food processor or liquidiser. Add the sugar, eggs and ground spices and blend to a smooth purée. Pour into the pastry cases and sprinkle the chopped ginger over the top. Cook for about 15 minutes until the filling is set. Leave to cool.

Whisk the cream, bourbon and sugar together until it forms soft swirls. Serve the pies at room temperature topped with spoonfuls of the whipped cream and a little chopped stem or glacé ginger.

Tip If you have butternut squash then this can be used instead, but make sure to weigh the squash after removing the seeds.

Tomato & pepper penne

These roasted vegetables are just as good added to cooked puy lentils, bulgar wheat or couscous. Serve hot or leave to cool and add to salad leaves.

Serves 4
Preparation time:
15 minutes
Cooking time:
25–30 minutes

4 different coloured
   peppers, quartered and
   de-seeded
700 g (1 lb 9 oz) **tomatoes**,
   halved if large
85 g (3 oz) **walnut halves**
3 **garlic cloves**, sliced
a small bunch of fresh **basil**
3 tablespoons **olive oil**
1 tablespoon **balsamic**
   vinegar
salt and freshly ground
   black pepper

To finish
400 g (14 oz) **penne** or
   macaroni
40 g (1½ oz) **butter**
fresh **basil**, to garnish
a little **olive oil**
grated **Parmesan cheese**,
   to garnish

Preheat the oven to 190°C/375°F/Gas Mark 5. Arrange the peppers with the skin sides uppermost in a roasting tin, add the tomatoes, walnut halves and garlic and tear the basil over the top. Drizzle with the oil and vinegar and season. Roast for 25–30 minutes until the peppers are browned.

When the vegetables are almost ready, bring a large saucepan of water to the boil, add the pasta and cook for 8–10 minutes or according to the packet directions until just tender.

Scoop the vegetables out of the roasting tin, reserving the pan juices. Remove the pepper and tomato skins with a knife and fork and then slice the peppers and roughly chop the tomatoes and walnuts.

Drain the pasta, return to the empty pan and toss with the butter and a little extra seasoning. Stir in the roasted vegetables and nuts and reserved pan juices. Spoon into bowls and top with extra basil leaves, a drizzle of olive oil and a little Parmesan.

Stuffed courgette flowers

Serve with salad leaves dressed with a little lemon juice and sprinkled with marigold petals or small nasturtium flowers.

Serves 4
Preparation time:
  25 minutes
Cooking time:
  12–16 minutes

250 g (9 oz) **ricotta cheese**
40 g (1½ oz) **Parmesan cheese**, finely grated
grated zest of ½ **lemon**
2 tablespoons chopped fresh **basil**
1 tablespoon chopped fresh **chives**
salt and freshly ground **black pepper**
12 **courgette flowers** with stems trimmed to about 2.5 cm (1 inch)
1 litre (1¾ pints) **sunflower oil**
sea salt

For the batter
115 g (4¼ oz) **self-raising flour**
25 g (1 oz) **cornflour**
1 **egg**
200 ml (7 fl oz) **sparkling mineral water**

Mix the cheeses together in a bowl and stir in the lemon zest, herbs and a little seasoning.

Open out each courgette flower a little, carefully remove the pistol and stamen and check for insects, taking care not to tear the flower. Spoon or pipe in the cheese mixture. The flower will expand as you add the stuffing, but try not to overfill them. Twist the tips of the petals to enclose the stuffing.

To make the batter, sift the flour and cornflour into a second bowl, add the egg and a little seasoning and gradually whisk in enough of the sparkling water to make a thin batter that will just coat your finger.

Pour the oil into a medium-sized saucepan and heat until it reaches 180°C/350°F on a sugar thermometer or the oil immediately bubbles around a drop of batter.

Twist the tips of the petals once more or stick together with a little batter. Dip three flowers in the batter, drain off any excess and then add the flowers to the hot oil. Cook for a few minutes until golden, turning over if needed, and then lift out with a slotted spoon. Put on a plate lined with kitchen towel and keep warm in the oven while cooking the remaining flowers in small batches.

Arrange on serving plates, sprinkled with a little sea salt.

Tip Try serving these with home-made tomato sauce.

Variation Other squash or pumpkin flowers can also be used.

Mixed roasted roots

A Sunday roast needn't just mean roast potatoes. Here, vegetables have been flavoured with fennel seeds, smoked paprika and olive oil.

Serves 4
Preparation time:
  25 minutes
Cooking time:
  45–60 minutes

450 g (1 lb) **potatoes**,
  scrubbed, halved and
  cut into wedges
4 tablespoons **olive oil**
1 teaspoon **fennel seeds**
½ teaspoon **smoked paprika**
salt and freshly ground
  black pepper
250 g (9 oz) **carrots**,
  scrubbed and halved
  lengthways
300 g (10½ oz) **parsnips**,
  peeled and cut into
  quarters lengthways
300 g (10½ oz) raw **beetroot**,
  peeled and cut into
  wedges

Preheat the oven to 190°C/375°F/Gas Mark 5. Add the potatoes to a saucepan of boiling water and parboil for 5 minutes. Tip into a colander, drain well and shake to rough up the edges.

Pour the oil into a roasting tin, add the fennel seeds and heat in the oven for 5 minutes. Sprinkle in the smoked paprika and some seasoning and then add the potatoes and all the remaining vegetables and turn in the oil.

Roast in the oven for 45–60 minutes, depending on the size of the vegetables, turning once or twice until golden.

Tip If you haven't used smoked paprika before, it is usually sold in small red tins and is sometimes called pimenton. It has a mellow, milder flavour than chilli powder. If you don't have any, add the same amount of paprika or a mix of paprika and chilli powder.

Baked honey carrots

Rather than losing all the flavour and nutrients into a pan of water, cook carrots in a roasting bag so they part-steam part-bake for a fuller flavour.

Serves 4
Preparation time:
   10 minutes
Cooking time:
   45–60 minutes

500 g (1 lb 2 oz) **carrots**
   (about 10 cm/4 inches
   long), scrubbed and
   halved lengthways
2 fresh **thyme sprigs**, plus
   extra to garnish (optional)
25 g (1 oz) **butter**
1 tablespoon **sherry vinegar**
2 teaspoons **runny honey**
4 tablespoons **chicken** or
   vegetable stock
salt and freshly ground
   black pepper

Preheat the oven to 190°C/375°F/Gas Mark 5. Place the carrots in a plastic roasting bag. Tear the thyme leaves from the stems straight into the bag and add the butter, vinegar and honey. Spoon in the stock, add a little seasoning, seal the bag and put on a baking tray.

Bake in the oven for 45–60 minutes until the carrots are just tender. Transfer the carrots and juices to a serving dish and sprinkle with a few extra thyme leaves, if using.

Tip If you don't have any roasting bags, tear off a large sheet of non-stick baking parchment or foil, fold in half then fold the edges of two of the sides over on themselves several times to make a bag. Add all the ingredients and then fold the remaining side over several times to enclose and seal. Transfer to a baking tray and cook as left.

Beetroot falafel

Although traditionally made with just chick peas and fried onions, the addition of grated beetroot adds the most amazing colour.

Serves 6
Preparation time:
  25 minutes
Cooking time:
  20 minutes

500 g (1 lb 2 oz) raw
  beetroot, peeled
1 tablespoon **olive oil**
1 **onion**, finely chopped
2 teaspoons **cumin seeds**,
  roughly crushed
1½ teaspoons **ground
  ginger**
300 ml (10 fl oz) **milk**
115 g (4¼ oz) **chick pea flour**
salt and freshly ground
  black pepper
410 g can **chick peas**,
  drained
1 litre (1¾ pints) **sunflower
  oil**

To serve
6 **pitta breads**
250 g (9 oz) **Greek yogurt**
mixed **salad leaves**
1 **red onion**, thinly sliced
fresh **mint** or **coriander
  leaves**

Coarsely grate the beetroot using a hand-held grater or a food processor fitted with a grating blade.

Heat the olive oil in a frying pan, add the onion and fry for a few minutes until just beginning to soften. Add the beetroot and fry for 5 minutes, stirring occasionally until tender. Add the cumin seeds and ginger and cook for 1 minute.

Pour the milk into a saucepan, bring just to the boil, add the chick pea flour and cook over a medium heat, whisking constantly until very thick and smooth. Season generously and then stir in the fried beetroot and onion mixture and the chick peas. Mix well and then spoon dessertspoonfuls on to a chopping board – aim to have 24 mounds.

Heat the sunflower oil in a medium-sized saucepan to a temperature of 60–180°C/ 325–350°F or until the oil bubbles around a small piece of falafel when it is added to the oil. Add the falafel, one by one, to the oil until about one-third are in the pan. Fry until browned and crisp. Lift out with a slotted spoon and put on a plate lined with kitchen towel. Continue until all the falafel are cooked.

Meanwhile, warm the pitta breads under the grill for a few minutes until hot and puffy. Split and fill the pittas with the falafels and spoonfuls of yogurt, the salad leaves, onion and herbs.

Tips Prepare beetroot wearing some rubber gloves or thin disposable latex gloves so that your hands don't become stained dark red.

These are also good served with the garlicky dip from the Root vegetable crisps (see page 64) instead of Greek yogurt.

Root vegetable crisps

Gourmet style crisps are expensive to buy, but if you have root vegetables in the garden they cost next to nothing to make yourself.

Serves 6
Preparation time:
15 minutes
Cooking time:
15 minutes

1 kg (2 lb 4 oz) mixed **root vegetables** (e.g. potatoes, carrots, parsnips and beetroot)
1 litre (1¾ pints) **sunflower oil**
sea salt

Dip
115 g (4¼ oz) **Greek yogurt**
115 g (4¼ oz) **crème fraîche**
2 **garlic cloves**, finely crushed
1 teaspoon **multicoloured peppercorns**, finely crushed
½–1 teaspoon **harissa paste**, to taste

Peel the vegetables, keeping the beetroot until last and ideally doing this on a separate chopping board or plate.

Cut the vegetables into long thin slices using a swivel-bladed vegetable peeler or mandolin or a food processor fitted with a thin metal slicing blade, again keeping the beetroot until last and as separate from the other vegetables as you can.

Mix all the ingredients for the dip together in a bowl.

Pour the oil into a medium-sized saucepan, heat until it reaches 180–190°C/350–375°F or until the oil bubbles around a vegetable slice dropped into the oil. Lower a slotted spoonful of vegetables into the hot oil, separate them and add a second spoonful, being watchful not to overcrowd the pan. Cook for a few minutes until golden around the edges and then scoop out of the pan with the spoon and drain well on kitchen towel.

Continue cooking the vegetable slices in small batches until they have all been cooked, leaving the beetroot to the end. Transfer to a serving plate with the dip and sprinkle with a little sea salt.

Tips Never leave a pan of hot oil unattended; if the phone rings, just leave it to ring.

The secret is to cut the vegetables very thinly, either with a swivel-bladed vegetable peeler, a mandolin or in a food processor with a thin slicing blade.

Potato & leek dauphinoise

This special potato dish can be prepared in advance and just popped in the oven at the last minute, making it ideal when friends come for supper.

Serves 4
Preparation time:
   10 minutes
Cooking time:
   30–40 minutes

650 g (1 lb 7 oz) **potatoes**, peeled and thinly sliced
150 g (5½ oz) **leeks**, thinly sliced
2–3 fresh **thyme sprigs**
2 **garlic cloves**, finely chopped
300 ml (10 fl oz) **double cream**
salt and freshly ground **black pepper**
25 g (1 oz) **butter**

Preheat the oven to 190°C/375°F/Gas 5. Add the potatoes to a saucepan of boiling water and cook for 3 minutes. Add the leeks, cook for 1 minute and then drain the potatoes and leeks well in a colander.

Tear the leaves from the thyme sprigs and mix with the garlic, cream and a generous amount of seasoning.

Transfer the potatoes and leeks to a buttered 1.4 litre (2½ pint) shallow ovenproof dish, tucking most of the leeks under the top layer of potatoes as they cook more quickly and have a tendency to overbrown.

Pour the cream mixture over the top and dot with the butter. Bake in the oven for 30–40 minutes until the top is golden brown and the cream has been mostly absorbed by the potatoes.

Tip Double cream may seem a little decadent but it adds the most wonderful richness that you just can't get with whipping cream.

Kartoffelphuffer

A German-inspired brunch dish. Delicious served with grilled bacon or smoked ham and a spoonful of soured cream.

Serves 4
Preparation time:
25 minutes
Cooking time:
12–15 minutes

25 g (1 oz) **butter**
3 sharp **dessert apples** or
  2 small **cooking apples**,
  cored and thickly sliced
2 tablespoons **cider vinegar**
2 tablespoons **runny honey**
650 g (1 lb 7 oz) **potatoes**,
  peeled and coarsely
  grated
1 **onion**, coarsely grated
115 g (4¼ oz) **self-raising**
  flour
salt and freshly ground
  black pepper
2 **eggs**, beaten
3–4 tablespoons **sunflower**
  oil

To serve
soured cream
4 slices **streaky bacon**

Heat the butter in a frying pan and fry the apples until just beginning to brown. Add the vinegar, honey and 2 tablespoons of water and cook for 3–4 minutes until syrupy and the apples are just tender. Take off the heat.

Pat the grated potatoes and onion dry with kitchen towel. Add to a mixing bowl, stir in the flour, plenty of seasoning and the beaten eggs and mix together.

Heat a little oil in a frying pan over a medium heat. Add heaped spoonfuls of the potato mix, leaving space between each mound, flatten slightly and fry until the undersides are golden. Turn the pancakes over and cook the other sides until golden and cooked through, adding a little extra oil if needed. Lift out of the pan and keep hot on a plate in the oven. Re-oil the pan and fry the rest of the mixture in the same way.

Meanwhile, grill the bacon until crispy. When ready to serve, reheat the apples, divide the pancakes between warmed plates and top with the apples, a spoonful of soured cream and a slice of bacon.

Tip If you have a food processor, fit the grating blade and you can grate the potato and onion in just a few seconds.

Hot marinated beetroot

Serve this while still hot with the Pickled courgette salad (see page 50) or with mixed salad leaves and smoked mackerel fillets.

Serves 4
Preparation time:
20 minutes +
30 minutes
marinating
Cooking time:
30–75 minutes

600 g (1 lb 5 oz) raw **beetroot**, scrubbed and leaves trimmed
4 tablespoons **olive oil**
4 tablespoons **red wine vinegar**
4 teaspoons **runny honey**
4 **garlic cloves**, thinly sliced (optional)
2 large pinches **chilli flakes**
salt and freshly ground **black pepper**
4 **star anise**

To garnish
baby beetroot leaves (optional)
baby red amaranth leaves (optional)

Place the beetroot in a saucepan, cover with cold water, bring to the boil and simmer for 30–75 minutes (see Tips) or until a knife can be inserted easily into the largest one.

Pour the oil and vinegar into a bowl, add the honey, garlic (if using), chilli flakes and seasoning and fork together to mix. Add the star anise and set aside.

Drain the cooked beetroot and then leave for 5–10 minutes until just cool enough to handle.

Peel away the skin and cut into 2 cm (¾ inch) cubes. Add to the dressing while still hot and toss together. Leave to stand for 30 minutes and serve while still warm, garnished with baby beetroot and amaranth leaves, if using.

Tips Don't trim the leaves too low down or the natural juices from the beetroot will leach into the water during cooking.

The cooking time will vary considerably depending on the size of the beetroot that you use; the smaller they are, the quicker they will take to cook.

Baby leek rarebit

Transform a few leeks into a main meal. As the sauce is so rich, serve simply with a few rocket leaves or wedges of tomato and some toast.

Serves 4
Preparation time:
  30 minutes
Cooking time:
  7–10 minutes

280 g (10 oz) mature
  Cheddar cheese, grated
3 tablespoons **plain flour**
1½ teaspoons **English
  mustard powder**
a pinch of **cayenne pepper**
2 teaspoons **Worcestershire
  sauce**
250 ml (9 fl oz) **light ale** or
  lager
500 g (1 lb 2 oz) young **leeks**,
  cut into 2 or 3 depending
  on size
100 g (3½ oz) **thick-sliced
  ham**
1 **egg**
1 **egg yolk**
4 tablespoons **coarse
  breadcrumbs**

Mix 225 g (8 oz) of the cheese, the flour, mustard powder and cayenne pepper together in a medium-sized saucepan. Add the Worcestershire sauce and gradually mix in the ale or lager. Transfer to the heat and bring to the boil, whisking until the cheese melts, the sauce thickens and any lumps have been removed. Set aside.

Arrange the leeks in the top of a steamer set over a saucepan of boiling water. Cover and cook for 5–8 minutes until the leeks are just tender. Preheat the grill to medium-high.

Wrap the ham around the leeks and arrange in a single layer in a shallow ovenproof dish.

Whisk the egg and egg yolk into the cheese sauce and pour over the leeks. Mix the remaining cheese and the breadcrumbs together and sprinkle over the top. Grill for 7–10 minutes until the topping is golden and the sauce is bubbling.

Variation Cauliflower can also be steamed and coated with the cheese sauce and finished with extra cheese and breadcrumbs before grilling and serving on wholemeal toast.

Carrot & parsnip soup

A comforting soup with a gentle chilli heat. For the best flavour, use a leftover chicken carcass to make home-made stock (see Tips).

Serves 4
Preparation time:
25 minutes
Cooking time:
35 minutes

2 tablespoons **olive oil**
1 **onion**, chopped
1 tablespoon **runny honey**
1 teaspoon **turmeric**
¼ teaspoon **chilli flakes**
350 g (12 oz) **carrots**, peeled and diced
350 g (12 oz) **parsnips**, peeled and diced
4 cm (1½ inch) fresh **root ginger**, peeled and finely chopped
1.2 litres (2 pints) **chicken** or **vegetable stock**
salt and freshly ground **black pepper**

To finish
150 g (5½ oz) **natural yogurt**
2 tablespoons **mango chutney**
a few mini **poppadoms** or **croûtons**

Heat the oil in a large lidded saucepan, add the onion and fry for 5 minutes, stirring from time to time until softened. Stir in the honey, turmeric and chilli flakes and fry for a minute or two until the onions are beginning to brown.

Add the diced vegetables and ginger and toss with the spiced onion. Pour over the stock, add a little seasoning and bring to the boil, stirring. Cover and simmer for 30 minutes or until the vegetables are tender.

Purée in batches in a food processor or liquidiser and return to the saucepan. Taste and adjust the seasoning if needed.

Reheat, ladle into bowls, swirl the yogurt over the top and drizzle with the mango chutney. Serve with mini poppadoms or croûtons.

Tips To make chicken stock, add a leftover chicken carcass from a roast chicken to a medium-sized saucepan, cover with cold water, add some seasoning and herb stalks, the trimmed tops from a couple of leeks or 1 quartered onion and 1 sliced carrot. Bring just to the boil, cover and simmer for at least 1 hour. Strain and use in soup, or cool and freeze for later use.

This soup also freezes well, so you might like to make up a double quantity, eat half and freeze the other half.

Variations Use this recipe as a base to make a spiced carrot soup, using just carrots instead of a mix of roots, or a parsnip and apple soup, adding 1 cooking apple and making the weight up to 700 g (1lb 9 oz) with parsnips. Omit the ginger and crumble in a little blue cheese at the end of cooking. Or try a beetroot and apple soup, omitting the honey, turmeric and ginger and flavouring with caraway seeds and paprika and serving with soured cream and chopped chives.

Fennel & pea couscous

A light fresh salad that can be served as it is or topped with grilled salmon or lamb chops. Cook the fennel on the barbecue or use a ridged frying pan.

Serves 4
Preparation time:
20 minutes
Cooking time:
8–10 minutes

200 g (7 oz) **couscous**
40 g (1½ oz) **currants**
salt and freshly ground
    black pepper
450 ml (16 fl oz) **boiling**
    water
115 g (4¼ oz) podded fresh
    peas
2 teaspoons **runny honey**
grated zest and juice of
    1 **lemon**
3 tablespoons **olive oil**
325 g (11½ oz) **fennel**
4 **spring onions**, cut into
    2–3 pieces
25 g (1 oz) **pine nuts**
100 g (3½ oz) **Feta cheese**
a few **pea shoots**, to garnish
    (optional)

Place the couscous, currants and some seasoning in a bowl, pour over the boiling water, cover with a plate and leave to stand for 5 minutes.

Add the peas to a saucepan of boiling water, cook for 3 minutes and drain, or leave raw if preferred.

To make the dressing, fork the honey, lemon zest and juice, oil and a little seasoning together in a medium-sized bowl.

To prepare the fennel, trim the green fronds from the top and reserve. Slice down through the top to the base and cut away the central core if large. Add to the dressing with the spring onions, toss until lightly coated and then scoop out with a slotted spoon and cook on a preheated barbecue or ridged griddle pan until browned and just tender. Reserve the dressing.

Chop the reserved green fronds from the fennel and add about 2 tablespoons to the soaked couscous with the reserved dressing, peas and pine nuts. Toss together and place in a serving dish. Spoon the griddled vegetables on the top, crumble over the Feta cheese and garnish with pea shoots. Serve while the vegetables are warm or leave to cool and then serve.

Tip If you are lucky enough to have asparagus in the garden, add a few stems to the dressing and barbecue or griddle with the other vegetables.

Cidered apple fritters

Fritters may seem like a relic of the 1950s, but here they get a modern makeover with cider in the batter and a side dish of gingered Greek yogurt.

Serves 4
Preparation time:
  25 minutes
Cooking time:
  10 minutes

250 g (9 oz) **Greek yogurt**
2 tablespoons chopped
  crystallised or **glacé**
  ginger
3 tablespoons **caster sugar**,
  plus extra for serving
150 ml (5 fl oz) **dry still**
  cider, plus an extra
  2 tablespoons
115 g (4¼ oz) **plain flour**,
  plus an extra
  2 tablespoons
6 small **dessert apples**
1 **egg**, separated
1 litre (1¾ pints) **sunflower**
  oil

Mix the yogurt with the ginger, 2 tablespoons of sugar and 2 tablespoons of cider, spoon into a serving dish and set aside.

Put the 2 tablespoons of flour on a plate. Peel and core the apples and cut into thick crossway slices with a hole in the centre. Lightly coat the apple slices with the flour.

Put the remaining flour and 1 tablespoon of sugar in a bowl and add the egg yolk. Whisk the egg white in a separate clean bowl until soft peaks form. Using the same whisk, beat the egg yolk into the flour and then gradually whisk in the remaining cider. Gently fold in the egg white.

Pour the oil into a saucepan and heat to 160–180°C (325–350°F) or until the oil immediately bubbles around a drop of batter. Shake off any excess flour from the apple slices, dip them one at a time into the batter and then drop them into the oil. Cook four or five apples slices at a time for a few minutes until the undersides are golden. Carefully turn over with a slotted spoon and remove from the oil when golden on both sides. Drain on kitchen towel. Continue dipping the remaining apples slices in batter and cooking in the oil until golden.

Dust with caster sugar and serve immediately with spoonfuls of the gingered yogurt.

Plum & rhubarb strudel

Ready-made filo pastry is very easy to use – the secret is unwrap it at the last minute so that it doesn't have the chance to dry out.

Serves 6
Preparation time:
 30 minutes
Cooking time:
 30–35 minutes

75 g (2¾ oz) **ground almonds**
55 g (2 oz) **caster sugar**
2 teaspoons **cornflour**
grated zest of 1 small
 orange
1 teaspoon **ground
 cinnamon**
250 g (9 oz) ripe **plums**,
 halved, stoned and sliced
250 g (9 oz) **rhubarb**, thickly
 sliced
270 g (9½ oz) frozen **filo
 pastry**, just defrosted
75 g (2¾ oz) **butter**, melted
icing sugar, sifted, for
 dusting
thick **double cream** or
 clotted cream, to serve

Preheat the oven to 190°C/375°F/Gas Mark 5. Mix the almonds, sugar, cornflour, orange zest and cinnamon together in a bowl, add the plums and rhubarb and stir together.

Unfold the filo pastry and lay two sheets together, slightly overlapping to make a 42 cm (16½ inch) square. Brush with a little of the butter and cover with two more sheets of pastry, arranged in the opposite direction to the first two, but again making a square. Brush again with a little more butter.

Spoon the fruit mixture in a long thick line about 7.5 cm (3 inches) up from the bottom edge and about 5 cm (2 inches) in from the ends. Fold the sides in over the filling then the bottom edge. Now roll the strudel from the bottom up to the top so that the filling is completely enclosed.

Transfer to a large non-stick baking tray and brush the outside with a little more butter. Wrap with the remaining filo pastry, torn into strips and slightly crumpled. Brush once more with the butter and bake for 30–35 minutes until golden. Check after 20 minutes and cover loosely with foil if the top looks as though it is browning too quickly.

Leave to stand for 10 minutes, dust heavily with icing sugar and cut into thick slices. Transfer to serving plates and serve warm with cream.

Tip A large strudel has been made here, but small mini strudels can also be made. Vary the filling depending on the fruits that you have – perhaps all plums, a mixture of plums and pears, or apples and sultanas.

Blackberry apple sorbet

This deliciously refreshing sorbet can be served on its own or with the Cidered apple fritters on page 76.

Serves 6
Preparation time:
 20 minutes + chilling
 + freezing
Cooking time:
 10 minutes

650 g (1lb 7oz) **Bramley apples**, peeled, quartered and cored
225 g (8 oz) **blackberries**
150 g (5½ oz) **caster sugar**
juice of 1 **lemon**
2 tablespoons chopped fresh **mint**

Slice the apples into a large lidded saucepan, add the blackberries, sugar and 300 ml (10 fl oz) of water, cover and bring just to the boil. Simmer gently for 10 minutes until the apples are soft.

Leave the fruit to cool in the pan and then purée the fruit and syrup in batches in a liquidiser or food processor until smooth.

Tip into a large sieve set over a bowl and press the purée through the sieve using the back of a spoon. Discard the seeds in the sieve. Stir the lemon juice and mint into the purée.

If making with an ice cream machine, chill the purée for 1 hour. Chill the ice cream machine as the handbook directs and then pour the purée into the machine and churn until thick enough to scoop (about 30–40 minutes). Serve now or spoon into a plastic container, cover and freeze until ready to serve.

To make in the freezer, pour the purée into a large non-stick or stainless steel roasting tin. Chill for 2–3 hours until frozen around the edges and still slightly slushy in the centre. (The larger the tin, the shallower the purée and the quicker it will freeze.) Mash with a fork to break up the ice crystals, transfer to a plastic container, cover and freeze overnight until firm.

Serve scooped into glasses or pretty tea cups. (You may need to leave the sorbet out for 10 minutes to make it soft enough to scoop.)

Variation To make apple crisps to serve with the sorbet, mix the juice from 1 lemon with 300 ml (10 fl oz) of water in a bowl. Thinly slice 2 dessert apples crossways straight into the water using a sharp knife or mandolin (no need to core or peel first). Toss gently in the water to help prevent the apples from browning and then drain well and arrange as a single layer on two baking trays lined with non-stick baking parchment. Sprinkle with 3 tablespoons of caster sugar and cook on the very lowest oven setting (80°C/175°F/Gas very low) for 2–3 hours until crisp. Leave to cool and then pack into a plastic box interleaving with non-stick baking parchment until needed. The crisps will store up to 1 week in a cool place.

Blackberry & apple clafoutis

These French-style puddings are made with a sweet Yorkshire pudding enriched with butter and sugar. Serve with cream or a scoop of ice cream.

Serves 4
Preparation time:
  15 minutes +
  30 minutes standing
Cooking time:
  25 minutes

55 g (2 oz) **plain flour**
25 g (1 oz) **caster sugar**
grated zest of ½ **lemon**
25 g (1 oz) **butter**, plus extra
  for greasing
1 **egg**
1 **egg yolk**
150 ml (5 fl oz) **half milk** and
  half water, mixed
½ teaspoon **vanilla essence**
3 small **dessert** or
  Bramley apples, peeled,
  quartered, cored and
  thinly sliced
115 g (4¼ oz) **blackberries**
icing sugar, sifted, for
  dusting

Sift the flour into a bowl and stir in the sugar and lemon zest. Melt the butter in a small saucepan and add to the flour with the egg and egg yolk. Add a little of the milk and water mixture, whisk together until smooth and then gradually whisk in the remaining milk and water mixture and the vanilla essence. Set aside for 30 minutes.

Preheat the oven to 190°C/375°F/Gas Mark 5. Liberally butter the base and sides of four 200 ml (7 fl oz) individual Yorkshire pudding tins. Pile the apples into the centre of the tins, sprinkling the blackberries over the top.

Stand the tins on a baking tray and cook for 5 minutes. Whisk the batter one more time and then quickly pour into the hot pudding tins so that the batter sizzles. Bake for about 20 minutes until well risen and golden. Dust with sifted icing sugar and serve immediately. (The puddings sink as they cool.)

Tip These also taste great made with stoned cherries, thickly sliced plums or sliced pears.

Pear chocolate brownies

Serve these squidgy brownies slightly warm with ice cream and a drizzle of warm chocolate sauce or leave to cool and serve with tea or coffee.

Makes 9 large squares
Preparation time:
30 minutes + cooling
Cooking time:
30–35 minutes

200 g (7 oz) **dark chocolate**, broken into pieces
200 g (7 oz) **butter**, diced
75 g (2½ oz) **hazelnuts**
3 just ripe **pears**, peeled, quartered, cored and sliced
3 **eggs**
200 g (7 oz) **caster sugar**
85 g (3 oz) **self-raising flour**
1 teaspoon **baking powder**

Preheat the oven to 180°C/350°F/Gas Mark 4. Line a 20 cm (8 inch) square cake or roasting tin with a large square of non-stick baking parchment, snipping diagonally into the corners so that the paper lines the base and sides of the tin.

Put the chocolate and butter in a bowl and set this over a saucepan of gently simmering water, making sure that the base of the bowl does not touch the water. Leave until the chocolate and butter are melted.

Add the hazelnuts to a dry frying pan and heat, shaking from time to time until lightly toasted. Add half the nuts and the pears to the lined tin and keep the rest to one side.

Whisk the eggs and sugar together for 3–4 minutes with an electric mixer until the mixture is thick and frothy (it needn't be so thick that the mixture leaves a trail). Gradually whisk in the melted chocolate and butter. Add the flour and baking powder and fold in gently.

Pour the chocolate mixture into the tin and ease into an even layer. Arrange the remaining nuts and pear slices randomly over the top. Bake for 30–35 minutes until well risen, the top is crusty and a knife comes out lightly smeared when inserted into the centre. Leave to cool and firm up.

Lift out of the tin using the paper and peel the paper away from the sides. Cut into squares and lift the brownies off the paper. Arrange on a plate to serve.

Tip Keep an eye on these towards the end of cooking; you are aiming for the centre to be slightly soft with a crisp crusty top and sides. Ovens vary too, so you might find that your brownies take a little longer or slightly less time to cook.

Toffee apples

It just wouldn't be a bonfire party without toffee apples. When cool, wrap in cellophane or non-stick baking parchment and tie with ribbons.

Serves 6
Preparation time:
   10 minutes
Cooking time:
   10 minutes

6 small **dessert apples**
6 **lolly sticks**
vegetable oil, for greasing
250 g (9 oz) **granulated**
   sugar
2 tablespoons **golden syrup**
1 tablespoon **white wine**
   vinegar
25 g (1 oz) **butter**

Wash and dry the apples carefully – if they are the slightest bit damp the toffee won't stick. Press a lolly stick into the top of each. Brush a little oil over a baking tray and set aside.

Pour the sugar into a medium-sized heavy based saucepan, add the golden syrup, 125 ml (4 fl oz) of water and the vinegar and cook over a low heat until the sugar has completely dissolved, stirring very gently once or twice to break up any clumps of sugar.

Increase the heat and boil the syrup, without stirring, until it just begins to caramelise and reaches 149°C (300°F) or the hard crack stage on a sugar thermometer. If you don't have a thermometer, take the pan off the heat and drop a little syrup into a cup of iced water. When the toffee is lifted out after a few seconds it will form brittle strands.

Take the pan off the heat, add the butter and swirl the pan slightly until the butter dissolves. Cool the toffee for a minute or two and then dip the apples one at a time into the toffee until completely coated. Lift out of the pan by the lolly stick, draining off the excess toffee, and transfer to the oiled baking tray. Continue until all the apples are coated, re-warming the toffee if it gets a little thick towards the last apple. Leave to cool and harden.

Tip These are best made on the day.

Variation Dry fry 40 g (1½ oz) of sesame seeds in a dry non-stick frying pan until golden and add with the butter for a coating rather like the Greek honey snacks known as pastelli.

Spiced apples & pears

Serve while still slightly warm with a spoonful of Greek yogurt or cool and freeze in small plastic boxes if you have a glut of fruit.

Serves 6
Preparation time:
10 minutes + cooling
Cooking time:
25–30 minutes

1 **orange**
1 **lemon**
85 g (3 oz) **light muscovado sugar**
1 **cinnamon stick**, halved
3 small **star anise**
1 kg (2¼ lb) mixed **Bramley apples** and **pears**

Pare the zest from the orange and lemon with a swivel-bladed vegetable peeler and cut into very thin strips. Halve the fruit, squeeze out the juice and discard the pips.

Add the juice and zest to a saucepan with 450 ml (16 fl oz) of water and the sugar and spices and heat gently, stirring occasionally, until the sugar has dissolved.

Peel, core and quarter the apples and pears and cut the apples into thick slices. Add to the syrup and simmer gently for 5 minutes or until the apple slices are just tender. Scoop the apple slices out of the pan with a slotted spoon and transfer to a serving bowl. Continue cooking the pears for 5–10 minutes more, or until just tender, and then scoop these out of the pan and add to the apples.

Boil the remaining syrup in the pan for 10 minutes until reduced to a thick syrup. Cool slightly and pour over the fruit. Leave to cool slightly. Serve when still warm or leave to go cold.

Tip Keep an eye on the apples as cooking apples quickly collapse if cooked too long. If you have dessert apples in the garden then you can use these instead, and if you don't have any pears then just use all apples.

Marmalade baked apples

Cooking apples are the usual choice for baking, but dessert apples are a more approachable size. Serve with ice cream or crème fraîche.

Serves 6
Preparation time:
 15 minutes
Cooking time:
 about 30 minutes

55 g (2 oz) **butter,** at room
 temperature
55 g (2 oz) **light muscovado
 sugar**
2 tablespoons **orange
 marmalade**
115 g (4¼ oz) ready-to-eat
 dried apricots, diced
85 g (3 oz) **raisins**
6 **dessert apples**

Preheat the oven to 180°C/350°F/Gas Mark 4. Cream the butter and sugar together in a bowl and then stir in the marmalade, dried apricots and raisins.

Cut a little off the base of each apple so that they stand upright and then cut a thicker slice off the top. Set the lids aside and core the centre of each apple. Stand in an ovenproof dish, pack the apricot mixture into the centre and over the top of each apple and add the apple lids.

Spoon 4 tablespoons of water into the base of the dish and bake, uncovered, for about 30 minutes, depending on the size of the apples, until tender. Transfer to serving dishes.

Apple tarte tatin

Bramley cooking apples are used here, but dessert apples are the traditional choice. Serve with spoonfuls of crème fraîche or vanilla ice cream.

Serves 6
Preparation time:
  30 minutes + cooling
Cooking time:
  30–35 minutes

85 g (3 oz) **butter**
1 **vanilla pod**, slit
  lengthways
115 g (4¼ oz) **granulated
  sugar**
pared zest and juice from
  ½ **orange** or **lemon**, cut
  into thin strips
4 **Bramley apples**, peeled,
  cored and cut into eight
300 g (10½ oz) **puff pastry**,
  defrosted if frozen

Preheat the oven to 200°C/400°F/Gas Mark 6. Melt the butter in a 20 cm (8 inch) frying pan with a metal handle. Scrape the seeds from the vanilla pod and add the seeds and pod to the butter. Add the sugar and citrus zest and heat gently until the sugar has dissolved. Toss the apple slices in the citrus juice, add to the pan and turn in the syrup. Remove the pan from the heat and make sure the apples are in an even layer with the vanilla pod underneath them.

Roll the pastry out thickly on a lightly floured surface to a 25 cm (10 inch) circle, using a plate as a guide. Lift the pastry over the rolling pin and drape over the surface of the apples. Tuck the edges of the pastry down the sides of the pan.

Make four small steam vents in the centre of the pastry with a small knife and bake the tart for 30–35 minutes until the pastry is well risen and buttery juices have begun to bubble up around the sides of the pan.

Take out of the oven and leave to cool for 10 minutes or so. Loosen the edges with a knife, cover the pan with a large plate, invert the pan on to the plate and remove. Cut into wedges, discarding the vanilla pod, and serve.

Tips If you don't have a metal-handled frying pan then transfer the butter and dissolved sugar mixture to a 20 cm (8 inch) round metal cake tin with a fixed base and then add the apples and pastry.

To make in advance, leave the cooked tart in the pan or cake tin, allow to cool and then warm through in the oven (still in the pan or tin) when almost ready to serve.

Strawberry crush

This can be made in advance and stored in the fridge. Try it for a healthy, effortless start to the day.

Serves 6
Preparation time:
  20 minutes + cooling
Cooking time:
  10 minutes

Muesli brittle
40 g (1½ oz) **butter**
3 tablespoons **thick set** or
  runny honey
50 g (1¾ oz) **light
  muscovado** or **caster
  sugar**
85 g (3 oz) **mixed seeds**
  (e.g. sesame, sunflower,
  pumpkin, golden linseeds
  or hemp seeds)
85 g (3 oz) **porridge oats**
40 g (1½ oz) **flaked almonds**
  or roughly chopped
  hazelnuts

Strawberry crush
450 g (1 lb) **strawberries**
2 tablespoons **thick set** or
  runny honey
750 g (1lb 10 oz) **natural
  yogurt**, to serve

To make the muesli brittle, preheat the oven to 180°C/350°F/Gas Mark 4. Heat the butter, honey and sugar in a saucepan until the butter has melted. Take off the heat and stir in the mixed seeds, oats and nuts. Tip on to an oiled baking tray and spread into an even layer.

Bake for 10 minutes until golden. Check after 5 minutes and, if the mixture seems to be browning more quickly around the edges, stir these into the centre and then continue cooking.

Leave to cool and harden. When cold, lift the brittle off the baking tray, break into pieces and transfer to a plastic container.

Mash or purée the strawberries with the honey and spoon into a plastic container. Chill the fruit purée and brittle in the fridge until required.

When ready to serve, spoon the fruit into bowls, swirl in the yogurt and top with the muesli brittle.

Variation Strawberries have been used here, but a mix of strawberries and raspberries or strawberries and plums could also be used. Or lightly cook some blackcurrants or blueberries with a little water and sugar or honey and cool and store in the fridge.

Blackcurrant fool

This light, rather old-fashioned dessert is very easy to make. If you are short of time, serve with shop-bought biscuits.

Serves 6
Preparation time:
  30 minutes + 2 hours chilling + cooling
Cooking time:
  20–25 minutes

450 g (1 lb) **blackcurrants**, stripped from stalks
2 tablespoons **blackcurrant cordial**
55 g (2 oz) **caster sugar**
300 ml (10 fl oz) **double cream**
135 g carton **low fat custard**
viola flowers, to decorate (optional)

Pistachio biscuits
2 **egg whites**
115 g (4¼ oz) **caster sugar**
55 g (2 oz) **butter**, melted
55 g (2 oz) **plain flour**, sifted
a few drops of **vanilla essence**
40 g (1½ oz) **pistachio nuts**, finely chopped
a little **icing sugar**, sifted, to decorate

Put the blackcurrants, cordial, sugar and 2 tablespoons of water into a saucepan, cover and cook gently for 5 minutes until the blackcurrants are softened. Purée in a liquidiser or food processor until smooth. Press through a sieve, discard the seeds and leave to cool.

Whip the cream in a bowl until it just forms soft swirls and then fold in the custard and the blackcurrant purée. Spoon into six small glasses and chill until needed.

To make the biscuits, preheat the oven to 200°C/400°F/Gas Mark 6 and line two baking trays with non-stick baking parchment.

Lightly whisk the egg whites in a clean bowl until frothy and then mix in the sugar. Gradually mix in the melted butter and then the flour until smooth. Add the vanilla essence and half the pistachio nuts.

Drop 6 teaspoons of the mixture, well spaced apart, on to each lined baking tray. Spread each spoonful into a thin round and sprinkle with a few extra nuts. Bake one baking tray for 4–5 minutes until the biscuits are just beginning to brown around the edges. Take it out of the oven and bake the second tray.

Leave the cooked biscuits to stand for a few seconds and then remove them from the tray with a palette knife. Repeat with the second baking tray and continue cooking small batches of biscuits until all the mixture has been used up. Leave to cool completely on a wire rack.

Lightly dust the biscuits with a little sifted icing sugar and serve with the fool, decorated with violas, if using.

Tip Make up extra when blackcurrants are at the height of their season. Freeze and then serve while still semi-frozen scooped into glasses and drizzled with a little crème de cassis, if you have some, for a refreshing cheats' ice cream.

Variation Blackberries can be used instead of the blackcurrants or try this with gooseberries with a little elderflower cordial, or rhubarb with a little chopped crystallised ginger instead of the cordial.

Summer berry tarts

These pretty little tarts could be topped with single fruits and then the warmed jelly brushed over the tops, if preferred.

Makes 12
Preparation time:
  40 minutes +
  30 minutes chilling +
  cooling
Cooking time:
  13–14 minutes

Pastry
175 g (6 oz) **plain flour**
40 g (1½ oz) **icing sugar**
85 g (3 oz) **butter**, at room
  temperature, plus extra
  for greasing
2 **egg yolks**

Filling
2 **egg yolks**
55 g (2 oz) **caster sugar**
20 g (¾ oz) **plain flour**
20 g (¾ oz) **cornflour**
300 ml (10 fl oz) **milk**
6 tablespoons **double cream**
½ teaspoon **vanilla essence**

Topping
4 tablespoons **redcurrant
  jelly**
450 g (1 lb) mixed **summer
  berries** (see Tip)

To make the pastry, add the flour to a mixing bowl, make a well in the centre and add the icing sugar, butter and egg yolks. Begin working the butter and egg yolks together with a wooden spoon, gradually mixing in the flour until the mixture can be squeezed together with your fingertips to make a soft dough. Chill for 15 minutes. Lightly grease 12 holes of a muffin tin with butter.

Roll the pastry out thinly on a lightly floured surface and stamp out 12 x 10 cm (4 inch) circles with a fluted biscuit cutter. Press into the muffin tin holes, rerolling the pastry trimmings and stamping out circles until all the pastry is used. Prick the bases with a fork and chill for 15 minutes.

Preheat the oven to 190°C/375°F/Gas Mark 5. Line each tart with a square of greaseproof paper and some baking beans and bake for 10 minutes. Remove the paper and beans and bake for 3–4 minutes until the bases are cooked and the tops are golden. Leave to cool.

To make the filling, place the egg yolks, sugar, plain flour and cornflour in a bowl and fork together until coarse crumbs form.

Pour the milk into a saucepan and bring just to the boil. Gradually whisk the milk into the egg yolk mixture until it is smooth and then pour it into the saucepan. Bring to the boil, whisking gently until it suddenly goes very thick. Keep whisking until smooth. Take the pan off the heat and beat in the cream and vanilla essence. Cover and leave to cool.

Transfer the tarts to a large plate and spoon in the custard. Gently warm the redcurrant jelly in a saucepan until just melted. Add the fruits, slicing any strawberries if they are large, and gently toss together. Spoon over the tarts and serve within 1 hour of finishing.

Tip Try using a mixture of raspberries, small strawberries, redcurrants or blackcurrants.

Double chocolate berry cake

A luxurious and slightly over the top cake that showcases home-grown fruit. Add candles for a birthday, or why not give instead of a birthday gift.

Serves 10
Preparation time:
25 minutes + cooling
Cooking time:
35–45 minutes

200 g (7 oz) **self-raising flour**
25 g (1 oz) **cocoa powder**
1 teaspoon **baking powder**
225 g (8 oz) **butter**, at room temperature, plus a little extra for greasing
225 g (8 oz) **caster sugar**
4 **eggs**
lemon geranium or **herb leaves**, to decorate (optional)

Filling
115 g (4¼ oz) **white chocolate**, broken into pieces
300 ml (10 fl oz) **double cream**
1 teaspoon **vanilla extract**
300 g (10½ oz) mixed fresh **raspberries, strawberries** (halved if large) and **redcurrants** (some still on their stalks)

Preheat the oven to 160°C/325°F/Gas Mark 3. Grease a 23 cm (9 inch) springform tin and line the base with a circle of greaseproof paper or non-stick baking parchment.

Sift the flour, cocoa and baking powder into a bowl. Cream the butter and sugar together in a mixing bowl with a wooden spoon, electric mixer or food processor if you have one.

Beat one egg into the butter and sugar mixture and then add a spoonful of the flour mix. Continue adding eggs and flour alternately until it has all been added and the mixture is smooth. Spoon into the tin and spread the top level. Bake for 35–45 minutes or until the top feels firm and a skewer comes out cleanly when inserted into the centre of the cake.

Leave to cool in the tin for 15 minutes and then loosen the edge and remove the springclip side. Loosen the base and transfer to a wire rack to cool completely.

When the cake is cold, place the white chocolate in a bowl and melt over a saucepan of barely simmering water. Whip the cream in a second bowl and then fold in the melted chocolate and the vanilla extract.

Peel the lining paper from the cake and cut the cake in half horizontally. Put one half on a serving plate, spoon over half the cream and sprinkle with half the berries (leaving the redcurrant strings for the top). Add the other cake half and top with the remaining cream and berries.

Decorate with a few leaves, if using, and cut into slices to serve.

Variation Instead of melted white chocolate and vanilla in the filling, you might also like to try some chopped mint and a little icing sugar.

Plum & almond cake

A moist deep almond cake. Serve warm with a spoonful of whipped cream for dessert or leave until completely cool and serve with cups of tea.

Serves 8
Preparation time:
 25 minutes + cooling
Cooking time:
 about 1¼ hours

225 g (8 oz) **butter**, at room
 temperature, plus a little
 extra for greasing
225 g (8 oz) **caster sugar**
4 **eggs**, beaten
225 g (8 oz) **self-raising flour**
55 g (2 oz) **ground almonds**
1 teaspoon **baking powder**
¼ teaspoon **almond
 essence**
grated zest of ½ **orange**
400 g (14 oz) just ripe **plums**,
 halved, stoned and thinly
 sliced
2 tablespoons **demerara
 sugar**
4 tablespoons **flaked
 almonds**
a little **icing sugar**, sifted,
 for dusting (optional)

Preheat the oven to 160°C/325°F/Gas Mark 3. Grease a 23 cm (9 inch) springform tin and line the base with a circle of greaseproof paper or non-stick baking parchment.

Cream the butter and sugar together in a mixing bowl with an electric mixer until light and fluffy. Gradually mix in alternate spoonfuls of beaten egg and flour until all have been added and the mixture is smooth. Mix the ground almonds with the baking powder and stir into the cake mixture with the almond essence and orange zest.

Spoon half the cake mixture into the prepared tin, smooth into an even layer and sprinkle with half the plum slices. Cover with the remaining cake mixture, smooth in place and arrange the rest of the plums on top. Sprinkle with the demerara sugar and flaked almonds.

Bake for about 1¼ hours until golden and a skewer comes out cleanly when inserted into the centre of the cake. Check after 45 minutes and cover the top loosely with foil if the flaked almonds seem to be browning too quickly.

Leave to cool in the tin for 20 minutes and then loosen the edge and remove the springclip side. Loosen the base and transfer the cake to a wire rack. Serve while still warm or leave to cool completely. Transfer to a plate, discarding the lining paper, dust with icing sugar, if using, and cut into wedges.

Variation A mixture of plums and the last of the raspberries also works well, or try it with diced cooking or dessert apples, a mix of apples and blackberries, or ripe pears.

Raspberry Trinity creams

This is said to have originated from Trinity College, Cambridge. Usually just flavoured with a vanilla pod, raspberries are added in this version.

Serves 6
Preparation time:
  20 minutes +
  30 minutes infusing
  + 4 hours chilling +
  cooling
Cooking time:
  30–35 minutes

1 **vanilla pod**
600 ml (20 fl oz) **double**
  cream
6 **egg yolks**
85 g (3 oz) **caster sugar**, plus
  6 tablespoons
200 g (7 oz) **raspberries**

Slit the vanilla pod along its length, scrape out the black seeds from the inside with a small knife and add to a medium-sized saucepan. Add the vanilla pod and cream and bring just to the boil. Leave to infuse for 30 minutes. Preheat the oven to 160°C/325°F/Gas Mark 3.

Whisk the egg yolks and 85 g (3 oz) of sugar together in a bowl until creamy. Remove the vanilla pod from the cream and discard and then bring the cream to the boil once more. Gradually mix into the egg yolks until smooth.

Divide the raspberries between six 250 ml (8 fl oz) shallow ovenproof dishes with a diameter of 9 cm (3½ inches) and a depth of 4.5 cm (1¾ inches) and stand the dishes in a roasting tin. Strain the vanilla cream over the top of the raspberries. Pour warm water into the roasting tin to come halfway up the sides of the dishes and bake the custards, uncovered, for 30–35 minutes or until just set in the centre with a slight wobble.

Lift the dishes out of the roasting tin. Allow to cool and then transfer to the fridge for at least 4 hours.

Sprinkle the tops with the remaining sugar and caramelise with a cook's blow torch. Leave to stand for 30 minutes or until ready to serve.

Tip If you don't have a cook's blow torch, put the dishes in the base of the grill pan, surround the dishes with ice and cook under a preheated grill with the tops of the dishes near the heat until golden. Put back in the fridge until ready to serve.

Raspberry muffins

Simply fork the ingredients together and bake for a weekend breakfast served straight from the oven with mugs of coffee or hot chocolate.

Makes 12
Preparation time:
  15 minutes + cooling
Cooking time:
  about 20 minutes

250 g (9 oz) **wholemeal flour**
100 g (3½ oz) **toasted wheatgerm**
150 g (5½ oz) **light muscovado** or **caster sugar**
2 teaspoons **baking powder**
1 teaspoon **bicarbonate of soda**
250 g (9 oz) **natural yogurt**
120 ml (4 fl oz) **sunflower oil**
3 **eggs**
2 teaspoons **vanilla essence**
200 g (7 oz) **raspberries**
3 tablespoons **sunflower seeds**

Preheat the oven to 200°C/400°F/Gas Mark 6. Line a 12 section muffin tin with paper cases or folded squares of non-stick baking parchment.

Place the flour, wheatgerm, sugar, baking powder and bicarbonate of soda in a large bowl and mix together.

Add the yogurt, oil, eggs and vanilla essence to a second smaller bowl and fork together. Add to the dry ingredients, fork together until only just mixed and then add the raspberries. Very briefly mix together.

Divide the mixture between the paper cases and sprinkle the sunflower seeds over the top. Bake for about 20 minutes until well risen and browned. Leave to cool for 10 minutes and serve warm.

Tip Freeze any extras for a healthy midweek breakfast; just defrost in the microwave.

Summer berry roulade

Definitely a pudding for a special occasion. For extra drama, dim the lights and add small party sparklers or wand candles.

Serves 8
Preparation time:
  30 minutes + 1 hour
  soaking + cooling
Cooking time:
  15 minutes

4 large **egg whites**
225 g (8 oz) **caster sugar**
1 teaspoon **cornflour**
1 teaspoon **white wine**
  vinegar
a few extra **berries** and
  borage flowers, to
  decorate
icing sugar, for dusting

Filling
450 g (1 lb) mixed sliced
  strawberries and whole
  raspberries
grated zest of ½ **orange**
grated zest of ½ **lemon**
2 tablespoons **caster sugar**
3 tablespoons undiluted
  Pimm's
300 ml (10 fl oz) **double**
  cream
150 g (5½ oz) **Greek yogurt**

Preheat the oven to 190°C/375°F/Gas Mark 5. Line a 33 × 23 cm (13 × 9 inch) Swiss roll tin or roasting tin with a large piece of non-stick baking parchment and snip diagonally into the corners so that the paper lines the base and sides and stands about 2.5 cm (1 inch) above the edges.

Whisk the egg whites in a large clean bowl until stiff, moist-looking peaks form and you can turn the bowl upside down without the egg whites moving. Gradually whisk in the sugar a teaspoonful at a time. Continue whisking for a minute or two once all the sugar has been added, until the meringue is very thick and glossy.

Mix the cornflour and vinegar together in a small bowl and fold into the meringue. Spoon into the lined tin and spread gently into an even thickness. Bake for 10 minutes.

Lower the oven temperature to 160°C/325°F/Gas Mark 3 and cook for another 5 minutes until the meringue is just firm to the touch, pale biscuit coloured and lightly cracked. Leave to cool for at least 1 hour.

Meanwhile, mix the berries with the orange and lemon zest, sugar and Pimm's and leave to soak for at least 1 hour.

Just before serving, place a tea towel on the work surface with a narrow edge facing you. Cover with a large piece of non-stick baking parchment and turn the meringue out on to the paper covered cloth. Peel the lining paper from the meringue base.

Whip the cream until it just forms soft swirls. Fold in the yogurt and juices from the summer fruit, spoon over the meringue and spread into a thin layer. Spoon the fruit over the top and roll the meringue up, starting from the bottom short edge and using the paper and tea towel to help.

Carefully transfer to a serving plate, removing the paper and cloth. Decorate with extra berries and borage flowers and dust with a little icing sugar. Serve cut into thick slices.

Tip Instead of the summer berries and Pimm's, use a little chopped mint and blackberries and raspberries, or raspberries and diced peaches, or diced plums.

Redcurrant cordial

Capture the flavours of summer in this easy cordial. Store in the fridge and dilute to taste with sparkling water or dry sparkling white wine.

**Makes 350 ml
(12 fl oz)
Preparation time:
20 minutes + 1 hour
standing + dripping
+ cooling
Cooking time:
40 minutes**

350 g (12 oz) **strawberries**, sliced
450 g (1 lb) **redcurrants**, stripped from their stalks
6 large fresh or dried **lavender heads** (optional)
about 175 g (6 oz) **granulated sugar**

Add the fruit to a saucepan with 150 ml (5 fl oz) of water and cook over a low heat for 10 minutes. Crush the fruit with a potato masher and continue to cook for a further 20 minutes until very soft. Crush once more to extract all the juice from the fruit.

Take the pan off the heat and add the lavender heads, if using. Leave to stand for 1 hour so that the lavender can flavour the berries.

Suspend a fabric jelly bag over a large jug, pour the fruit mixture into the bag and leave to drip for an hour or so.

Measure the juice, and for each 300 ml (10 fl oz) allow 175 g (6 oz) of sugar. Add the juice and sugar to a saucepan, heat gently until the sugar has dissolved and then simmer for 5 minutes until syrupy.

Pour into a clean dry bottle, seal and leave to cool. Store in the fridge until required.

Tip For long-term storage of the syrup, pour into sections of an ice cube tray, freeze until firm and then press out of the tray and store in a sealed plastic bag. Defrost as many as you need when necessary.

Raspberry & lemon cakes

If you don't have individual loaf tins, bake in 12 paper cases in sections of a muffin tin, reducing the cooking time to 12-15 minutes.

Makes 6
Preparation time:
   25 minutes + cooling
Cooking time:
   20–25 minutes

vegetable oil, for greasing
115 g (4¼ oz) **butter**, at room
   temperature
175 g (6 oz) **caster sugar**
175 g (6 oz) **self-raising flour**
2 **eggs**
grated zest and juice of
   1 **lemon**
115 g (4¼ oz) **raspberries**
115 g (4¼ oz) **granulated**
   sugar

Preheat the oven to 180°C (350°F) Gas Mark 4. Brush six individual metal loaf tins, each 10 × 5 × 3 cm (4 × 2 × 1¼ inches) or 175 ml (6 fl oz), with a little vegetable oil and line the base and two long sides of each with a strip of greaseproof paper or non-stick baking parchment.

Cream the butter and caster sugar together in a bowl with a wooden spoon or electric mixer. Add a little of the flour and one egg, beat again and repeat. Add the remaining flour and beat until smooth.

Beat in the lemon zest and divide the mixture equally between the lined tins. Press the raspberries into the cake mixture and spread the mixture into even layers. Bake for 20–25 minutes until golden, well risen and a skewer comes out cleanly when inserted into the centre of the cakes.

While the cakes cook, mix the lemon juice with the granulated sugar. As soon as the cakes come out of the oven, spoon over the lemon syrup and then leave to cool for 10 minutes. Loosen the edges of the cakes and lift out of the tins by holding the lining paper. Leave to cool on a wire rack.

Very berry jelly

Amazingly fresh and fruity, this vibrant softly set jelly doesn't need the adornment of cream or ice cream – just serve 'au natural'.

Serves 4
Preparation time:
  25 minutes + 4 hours chilling
Cooking time:
  10 minutes

450 g (1 lb) mixed **summer fruits** (e.g. raspberries, strawberries and redcurrants)
85 g (3 oz) **caster sugar**
4 **gelatine sheets**, each
  12 × 7 cm
  (4½ × 2¾ inches)
225 g (8 oz) **strawberries**, sliced
85 g (3 oz) **redcurrants**
redcurrant strings, a few extra small **strawberries** or **herb flowers**, to decorate

Add the mixed summer fruits to a saucepan with the sugar and 300 ml (10 fl oz) of water. Simmer, uncovered, for 10 minutes, stirring and breaking up the fruit with a wooden spoon until soft.

Put the gelatine leaves in a shallow dish and just cover with cold water. Leave to soften for a few minutes.

Strain the hot fruit juice into a bowl, keeping the soft fruit in the sieve. Lift the soaked gelatine leaves out of the water, add to the hot fruit juice and stir until completely dissolved.

Purée the cooked fruit in a liquidiser or food processor, press through a sieve into the gelatine mixture and discard the seeds.

Stir the fruit syrup and leave to cool. Pour into four pretty glasses and add the sliced strawberries and extra redcurrants. Chill in the fridge for 4 hours until very lightly set and then decorate the tops with redcurrant strings, halved strawberries or herb flowers.

Index